The American Revolution
A PICTURE SOURCEBOOK

by John Grafton

DOVER PUBLICATIONS, INC.
NEW YORK

Published in Canada by General Publishing Company, Ltd.,
30 Lesmill Road, Don Mills, Toronto, Ontario.
Published in the United Kingdom by Constable and Company,
Ltd., 10 Orange Street, London WC 2.

The American Revolution: A Picture Sourcebook is a new
work, first published by Dover Publications, Inc., in 1975.

DOVER *Pictorial Archive* SERIES

The American Revolution: A Picture Sourcebook belongs to
the Dover Pictorial Archive Series. Up to ten illustrations
from this book may be reproduced on any one project or in
any single publication, free and without special permission.
Wherever possible include a credit line indicating the title of
this book and publisher. Please address the publisher for permission to make more extensive use of illustrations in this
volume than that authorized above.
The republication of this book in whole is prohibited.

International Standard Book Number: 0-486-23226-3
Library of Congress Catalog Card Number: 75-19500

Manufactured in the United States of America
Dover Publications, Inc.
180 Varick Street
New York, N.Y. 10014

INTRODUCTION

American history begins so recently that the American Revolution is the only major war in our history of which we have no photographic record. For that obvious reason, our collective pictorial memory of the events of the Revolutionary era has been totally shaped and conditioned by the work of a very mixed group of creative artists. Some lived during the Revolution, many did not; some created masterpieces crucial to the history and development of American art; others were only moderately competent, minor artists who just happened to devote themselves to this period and subject. This book represents an attempt to gather in one place, and wherever possible in a form suitable for easy reproduction from these pages, many of the best-known and most familiar pictures and images of the American Revolution as they have come down to us over the two centuries since 1776. In no way is this a history of the American Revolution; only enough text has been supplied to place each picture within the context of events. So much art has been available to us, however, that it has been possible to arrange the pictures according to the chronology of the Revolution; the result is a kind of connected pictorial narrative with which it is possible to follow the history of the Revolution from the Stamp Act of 1765 to the disbanding of the Continental Army in 1783. In a supplementary section some additional material on the people and life of the Revolutionary period has been supplied.

In the broad category of work by men who lived during the Revolution, this book includes reproductions of some of the best and most influential work of a most distinguished group of artists. Our image of Washington, for example, has always been and always will be Gilbert Stuart's Washington. Our conception of what it was like to be in the Pennsylvania State House when the Continental Congress debated and finally declared independence from England will always be based on what is certainly John Trumbull's most famous painting. Beyond this realm of fine art, however, the Revolutionary era has also left us a sizable amount of less ambitious but not less interesting work produced by men who lived during the events they depicted. The unfortunate Major André, for example, devoted part of his last day to sketching a fine self-portrait. Paul Revere left us engravings which themselves became a part of the political process, having timely propaganda value, as well as being milestone achievements in the young history of American printmaking. Amos Doolittle and Ralph Earle gave us a crucial series of engravings of Lexington and Concord, crude art, but vital and fascinating pictures produced by participants in the drama they attempted to record. These are only a few examples of the kind of material included here; also included is the work of too often anonymous sketchers, typographers, and printers who left us drawings, newspapers, handbills, broadsides, engraved medals and illustrated books, all of which form a part of the immediate pictorial record of the Revolution.

The question of historical accuracy must always enter into a discussion of art produced long after the events pictured, and some of the nineteenth-century art and illustration included here may be questioned on these grounds. However, doubts about its accuracy should not keep us from enjoying such work, or understanding its importance to the way our images of the Revolution have been shaped. Also, much of it is accurate indeed—in many cases more accurate than much of the art actually produced during and shortly after the Revolution by men who lived through it. The nineteenth-century work reproduced in this book is quite varied. The crude woodcuts of John W. Barber, produced not long after the Revolution, were executed without much conception of accurate representation of events. The vast output of America's first great book illustrator, Felix O.C. Darley, was often romantic but also often very true-to-life—the work of a man who obviously knew a great deal about the life of the historical period he was drawing. The immense image of Washington crossing the Delaware by Emanuel Leutze was truly a work of the imagination, but is still an image indelibly stamped on our pictorial consciousness of the Revolution. There are the sharp wood engravings of the indefatigable Benson Lossing, who traveled thousands of miles in the 1840's to sketch for himself the remains of battle scenes and battles then only seventy years past. Numerous historical scenes and portraits were exactingly executed by the prolific Alonzo Chappel, who despite his large output remains a somewhat nebulous figure in the history of nineteenth-century popular American art. Finally we have running through this book the work of the outstanding group of American periodical illustrators of the later nineteenth century, dominated by Howard Pyle, several of whose best-known Revolutionary drawings — dramatic, accurate, and forceful like all his best work—are included here. It is hoped that the combined efforts of this large roster will work together, for the reader who wants to try to answer for himself the only ultimately unanswerable but most fascinating question about the American Revolution—what did it look like?

New York   JOHN GRAFTON
August, 1975

The TIMES are
Dreadful
Doleful
Dismal
Dolorous, and
DOLLAR-LESS.

THE PENNSYLVANIA JOURNAL;
AND
WEEKLY ADVERTISER.

Thursday, October 31. 1765

NUMB 1195

EXPIRING: In Hopes of a Resurrection to LIFE again.

I am sorry to be obliged to acquaint my readers that as the Stamp Act is feared to be obligatory upon us after the *first of November* ensuing (The Fatal To-morrow), The publisher of this paper, unable to bear the Burthen, has thought it expedient to stop awhile, in order to deliberate, whether any methods can be found to elude the chains forged for us, and escape the insupportable slavery, which it is hoped, from the last representation now made against that act, may be effected. Mean while I must earnestly Request every individual of my Subscribers, many of whom have been long behind Hand, that they would immediately discharge their respective Arrears, that I may be able, not only to support myself during the Interval, but be better prepared to proceed again with this Paper whenever an opening for that purpose appears, which I hope will be soon.
WILLIAM BRADFORD.

Adieu Adieu to the LIBERTY of the PRESS.

THE STAMP ACT OF 1765. FIG. 1: Reply to the Stamp Act in William Bradford's *Pennsylvania Journal*, including a caricature of the stamp in the upper right corner. FIGS. 2–3: Facsimiles of the revenue stamps which had to appear on virtually every sort of publication including legal and commercial papers and licenses. FIG. 4: New Yorkers burning seized stamped papers as later pictured by A. B. Frost. FIG. 5: A Stamp Act official attacked and beaten by irate citizens.

6

7

8

THE STAMP ACT OF 1765 *(Continued)*. Fig. 6: A common scene in the winter of 1765-66, a Stamp Act official hanging in effigy. Fig. 7: Another view of such a scene. Fig. 8: Howard Pyle's drawing from *Harper's Magazine,* March, 1882, shows an angry mob attempting to force a stamp officer to resign.

9

LEADERS OF THE COLONISTS. Fig. 9: Patrick Henry, after a portait by J. B. Longacre. The Virginia-born orator led that colony's opposition to the Stamp Act and subsequent measures from the time he delivered his "If this be treason" speech in that cause to the Virginia House of Burgesses (Fig. 11). Fig. 10: James Otis, from a painting by Alonzo Chappel. Boston lawyer Otis was the intellectual leader of Massachusetts' opposition to the English colonial tax measures after his 1761 court battle against the "writs of assistance" or general search warrants which Crown officials used to search for smuggled goods. Fig. 12: The Raleigh Tavern in Williamsburg, meeting-place of Virginia patriots.

10

11

12

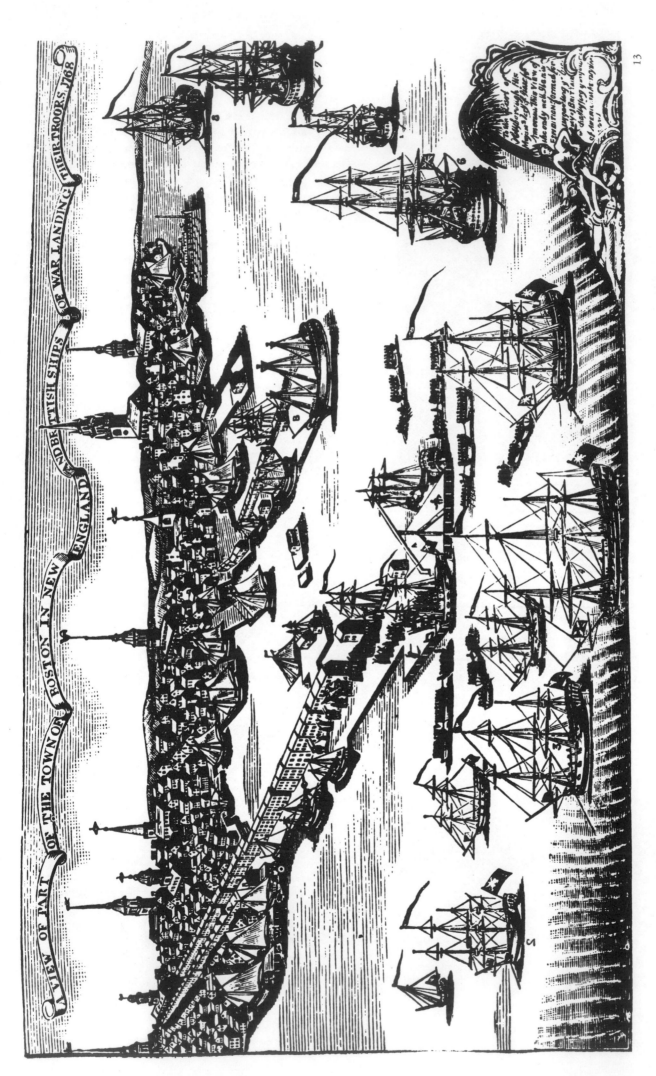

A VIEW OF PART OF THE TOWN OF BOSTON IN NEW ENGLAND AND BRITISH SHIPS OF WAR LANDING THEIR TROOPS. 1768.

THE OCCUPATION OF BOSTON. Fig. 13: Paul Revere's engraving, issued in 1770, of the landing of British troops in Boston on October 1, 1768. The engraving showing the fleet of huge British ships landing troops of the Fourteenth and Twenty-ninth Regiments on Boston's Long Wharf carried the insolently sarcastic inscription: "To the Earl of Hillsborough, His Majesty's Secy. of State for America This View of the only Well Plan'd Expedition formed for supporting ye Dignity of Brittain & chastising ye insolence of America, is humbly Inscribed."

Engrav'd Printed & Sold by PAUL REVERE BOSTON

THE BOSTON MASSACRE. Fig. 14: Paul Revere's engraving of the Boston Massacre of March 5, 1770, was an obvious and effective piece of colonial propaganda. The soldiers are shown firing at the raised-sword command of their leader on a peaceful, defenseless and respectable group of citizens far removed from the actual rock- and ice-throwing mob of toughs, many of whom came to the scene armed with clubs and other weapons. The rifle barrel which can barely be seen protruding from the window on the right was a complete fabrication. This most famous of early American prints was actually copied by Revere from a more elaborate engraving by an artist named Henry Pelham, and a letter from Pelham to Revere, justifiably bitter over the plagiarism, was later found in London's Public Record Office.

THE BOSTON MASSACRE. Fig. 15: The survival of Revere's imagery may be seen in this 1855 illustration from *Ballou's Pictorial Drawing-Room Companion*. Fig. 16: Hostile Bostonians greet a troop of British soldiers at the waterfront. Fig. 17: Howard Pyle's version of the Massacre appeared in *Harper's Magazine,* August, 1883.

19

20

21

FIG. 18: A contemporary broadside gives evidence of popular reaction to the Boston Massacre and similar incidents. The list of victims of course includes the last name of Crispus Attucks, a black man killed by the British. FIG. 19: British troops in Boston enduring the taunts of local boys. FIG. 20: This later drawing by Felix O. C. Darley captures a tense moment after the shooting on March 5. Note, beside the fallen hat of the victim, the wooden club, no doubt the weapon he had been carrying a moment before. A similar stick is also visible in Pyle's version (FIG. 17). FIG. 21: Faneuil Hall, meeting-place of Bostonians.

THE BOSTON TEA PARTY. Fɪɢ. 22: This panoramic view of the Boston Tea Party by John An-

drew appeared in *Ballou's Pictorial* in 1856. It represents the scene at Griffin's Wharf, Boston, on the night

22

of December 16, 1773, when a band of Bostonians, thinly disguised as Indians, boarded three British tea ships and threw overboard 342 chests of tea in protest against the British attempt that year to tax American tea consumption.

23

To the Public.

THE long expected TEA SHIP arrived laſt night at Sandy-Hook, but the pilot would not bring up the Captain till the ſenſe of the city was known. The committee were immediately informed of her arrival, and that the Captain ſolicits for liberty to come up to provide neceſſaries for his return. The ſhip to remain at Sandy-Hook. The committee conceiving it to be the ſenſe of the city that he ſhould have ſuch liberty, ſignified it to the Gentleman who is to ſupply him with proviſions, and other neceſſaries. Advice of this was immediately diſpatched to the Captain ; and whenever he comes up, care will be taken that he does not enter at the cuſtom-houſe, and that no time be loſt in diſpatching him.

New-York, April 19, 1774.

24

TEA AND THE AMERICAN REVOLUTION. FIG. 23: Another view of the Boston Tea Party. Resistance to British tea quickly became a cause throughout the colonies. FIG. 24: Proclamation from New York relating how a tea ship was prevented from landing in New York in 1774. FIG. 25: A British cartoon of 1774 was designed to show how Royal authority was disregarded in Boston. British tea is being forced down the tarred and feathered tax collector while the "Stamp Act" is nailed upside down to the Liberty Tree. A noose is ready for the collector while the Boston Tea Party takes place in the background. FIG. 26: Darley's L-shaped sketch represents the progress of events from the hanging of Stamp Act officials in effigy, to the Boston Massacre, the Tea Party and, yet to come for the colonists, armed conflict. FIG. 27: Another contemporary cartoon shows America, designated by the Indian headdress, forced to take British tea.

25

26

27

28

29

PHILADELPHIA.

In CONGRESS, Thursday, September 22, 1774.

RESOLVED,

THAT the Congreſs requeſt the Merchants and Others, in the ſeveral Colonies, not to ſend to Great Britain any Orders for Goods, and to direct the execution of all Orders already ſent, to be delayed or ſuſpended, until the ſenſe of the Congreſs, on the means to be taken for the preſervation of the Liberties of *America,* is made public.

An Extract from the Minutes,
CHARLES THOMSON, *Sec.*

Printed by *W.* and *T. BRADFORD.*

30

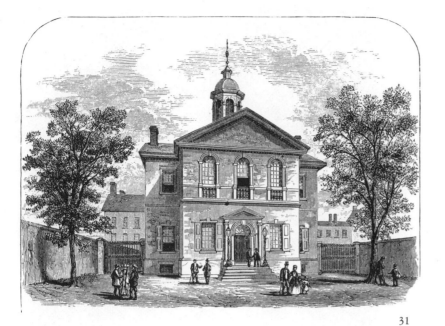

31

32

33

TOWARD REVOLUTION. FIG. 28: Engraving of George III, from a portrait by Sir Thomas Lawrence. FIG. 29: Edmund Burke, British statesman and opponent of the Crown's policies toward America. This engraving is from a portrait by Sir Joshua Reynolds. FIG. 30: Proclamation issued by Congress as it moved toward a policy of total non-importation of British goods during the autumn of 1774. FIG. 31: Carpenters' Hall, Philadelphia, site of the First Continental Congress in September, 1774. FIG. 32: This cartoon of a rattlesnake cut in segments representing parts of America with the legend "Join, or Die" was designed by Benjamin Franklin at the time of the Albany Congress of 1754 (the issue then was joint action with regard to the Indians, not the British) and first published in Franklin's *Pennsylvania Gazette* on May 9, 1754. FIG. 33: An early variant of Franklin's cartoon. FIG. 34: In the years just before the Revolution the cartoon was still in circulation in somewhat altered form. Here we can see that another segment, representing Georgia, has been added and the legend altered to "Unite or Die." FIG. 35: Even before the Albany Congress, Franklin had been inspired to use the rattlesnake as an American image. In 1751 he facetiously proposed that rattlesnakes be collected and exported to England, in return for the convicts which the British were transporting to the colonies. Franklin's sardonic championing of the rattlesnake struck home. The snake appears on an early American naval flag, and in this figure we see it used in a device published in 1774 as a symbol of American unity.

34

35

36

37

38

39

LEXINGTON AND CONCORD. FIG. 36: Paul Revere, from a portrait by Gilbert Stuart. In addition to his work as silversmith, engraver, master propagandist and leader of the Boston Tea Party, Revere was the principal express rider for the Boston Committee of Safety. FIG. 37: Samuel Adams, from a portrait by John Singleton Copley. Adams was no doubt the most influential spokesman among the people of Boston in the years before the Revolution and one of the first in the colonies to commit himself to independence. John Adams was his second cousin. FIG. 38: John Hancock, from a Copley portrait. Hancock, the richest man in Boston before the Revolution, was President of the Second Continental Congress and the first to sign the Declaration of Independence. FIG. 39: Hancock's house in Boston, one of the most imposing colonial mansions.

40

42

43

FIG. 40: An alarm bell of the type used in New England towns to summon the militia to Concord. FIG. 41: A device possibly engraved by Paul Revere and widely circulated in the colonies during the furor over the Boston Port Bill of 1774 which completely closed the port of Boston to all shipping. The device shows a skull and crossbones between a Crown and a Liberty Cap, signifying perhaps the battle to the death between the Crown and Liberty. FIG. 42: Revere and other post riders often used handbills to spread news among the towns around Boston. FIG. 43: An anonymous artist's conception of Revere's famous ride on the night of April 18, 1775. FIG. 44: Darley's drawing of Revere bringing news of the British troop movement to Lexington. In addition to rousing the militia to protect the military stores at Concord which the British troops had set out to seize, Revere's goal was to warn Hancock and Samuel Adams, who were in hiding from the British in a Lexington parsonage. Revere delivered his message at Lexington, but was captured by a small British advance force between there and Concord. Other riders continued to spread the word, however, and Revere himself was soon released.

41

44

45

48

46

47

LEXINGTON AND CONCORD *(Continued)*. FIGS.
45–47: Three scenes by Darley of the New England
Minutemen. FIG. 45: Manufacturing rifles. Early in the
war the Americans' home-made weapons put them at a
disadvantage compared to more sophisticated British
weaponry. FIG. 46: A Minuteman behind his plow, ready
to move out with his weapon on a moment's notice. FIG.
47: A Minuteman leaving for action, as a minister be-
stows his blessing. FIG. 48: Howard Pyle's drawing of
Paul Revere at Lexington, from *Harper's Young People*,
May 10, 1889. FIGS. 49–50: Darley's drawings of a
Minuteman preparing for battle and a rider giving the
call to arms.

49

50

17

52

51

53

LEXINGTON AND CONCORD *(Continued)*. Fig. 51: Minutemen from a nearby Massachusetts town prepare to leave for Lexington after receiving the first battle alarm. Fig. 52: A Darley variant of this scene. Fig. 53: Howard Pyle's drawing of the action at Lexington from *Harper's Magazine,* October, 1883. Lexington, 11 miles northwest of Boston, was on the road the British troops had to take to capture the arms depot at Concord. Roughly eighty militiamen appeared against 700 British regulars. The consensus now is that before the colonials could disperse, which they were in the act of doing, someone fired a shot which was followed by a volley from the British, leaving eight colonials dead and ten wounded. The real battle then took place at Concord, eight miles away.

FIG. 54: A nineteenth-century engraving of the battle of Lexington, April 19, 1775. This illustration shows the colonials at center and left returning the fire of the British regulars. The evidence is that the British sustained only a few casualties at Lexington, with none killed (one of the wounded was the British Commander Pitcairn's horse) ; this picture must therefore be considered largely fanciful, dramatic as it is.

LEXINGTON AND CONCORD *(Continued)*. FIG. 55: The house of Reverend Jonas Clark at Lexington where Adams and Hancock stayed the night before the battle. FIG. 56: A John W. Barber woodcut illustrating the battle at Lexington. FIG. 57: As the events of April 19 unfolded, riders like the one pictured continued to spread the call for militia throughout Massachusetts and even into neighboring New England states and New York. FIG. 58: Darley's conception of the action at Lexington.

The Battle of Lexington, April 19th 1775. Plate I

1. Major Pitcairn, at the head of the Regular Grenadiers.
2. The Party, who first fired on the Provincials at Lexington.
3. Part of the Provincial Company of Lexington.

4. Regular Companies on the road to Concord.
5. The Meetinghouse at Lexington.
6. The Publick Inn.

A. Doolittle. Sculpt.

FIGS. 59–62: The four illustrations on this and succeeding pages are a series on the action at Lexington and Concord designed by an artist named Ralph Earle and engraved by a Connecticut militiaman, Amos Doolittle, who was on the scene a few days after the fighting. FIG. 59: The Lexington militia are dispersing after a volley from the front rank of British troops. Major Pitcairn is on horseback, directing his troops.

Plate II A View of the Town of Concord

1 Companies of the Regulars marching into Concord.
2 Companies of Regulars drawn off in order.
3 A Detachment of destroying the Provincial Stores.
4 & 5 Colonel Smith & Major Pitcairn viewing the Provincials
who were mustering on an East Hill in Concord
6 The Townhouse 7 The Meetinghouse

60

LEXINGTON AND CONCORD (Continued). Fig. 60: Pitcairn and Lt. Col. Francis Smith reconnoiter from the cemetery at Concord as their troops march into the town below them.

Plate III : The Engagement at the North Bridge in Concord.

1 · *The Detachment of the Regulars who fired first* 2 · *The Provincials headed by Colonel Robinson &* *on the Provincials at the Bridge* *Major Buttrick* 3 · *The Bridge*

A. Doolittle Sculp.

FIG. 61: At Concord, the British, on the right, begin their retreat after the battle at North Bridge.

23

Plate IV.   A View of the South Part of Lexington.

1. Colonel Smiths Brigade retreating before the Provincials.
2. Earl Percys Brigade meeting them.
3. & 4. Earl Percy & Col Smith.   5.Provincials.
6 & 7. The Flanch guards of Percys Brigade.
8. A Field piece pointed at the Lexington Meetinghouse.
9. The Burning of the Houses in Lexington.

A. Doolittle sculp.

LEXINGTON AND CONCORD (Continued). FIG. 62: British columns, in center, converge to continue their retreat as the militiamen harass them, in foreground, from behind a stone wall. Modern historians have questioned some details in the Doolittle plates, but the over-all view they give of the action seems reasonably accurate.

63

64

65

66

CONCORD. FIG. 63: Scene at Concord's North Bridge where Isaac Davis, a colonial militia leader, was killed. Both sides lost men at the bridge and the British were forced to return toward Boston. FIG. 64: Colonials removing the military stores from Concord, preventing their capture by the British. The major part of the stores were removed before the first British column arrived at Concord. FIG. 65: Darley's sketch of the action at Concord. FIG. 66: Benson Lossing drew this sketch of the battleground at Concord roughly seventy-five years after the battle.

RETREAT OF THE BRITISH FROM CON-
CORD. Fig. 67: Engraving after a painting of the retreat of the British from Concord by Alonzo Chappel.
Chappel's paintings of battle scenes are generally very
accurate in conception and detail and much more interesting than his often rather flat historical portraits. In the
scene above, the British are retreating down the main road
while being harassed from both sides by irregular groups
of militia. British losses for the day totaled 73 killed and
174 wounded; the colonials lost 49 men and had 41
wounded.

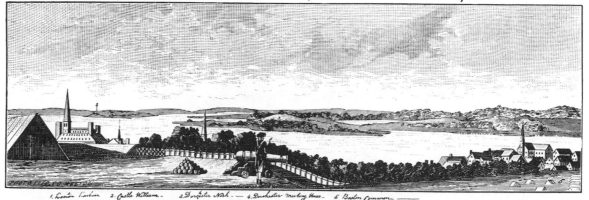

1. Boston Harbour.   2. Castle William.   3. Dorchester Neck.   4. Dorchester meeting house.   5. Boston Common.   68

Nº 2   and Redouts of his Majesties Troops.— NB. These Views were taken by Lt Williams, of the R: W Fuziliers & copied from a Scetch of the Original Drawing

6. Boston Common.   7. Our Lines.   8. The Block House on the Neck.   9. Rebels Intrenchments.   10. Roxbury meeting house.   11. Rebels Intrenchments.   12. Encampment of the Rebels.   13. Hancock's house.   69

Nº 3   by Lt Wood of the same Regiment.— The Original Drawings are now in the possesion of the King.

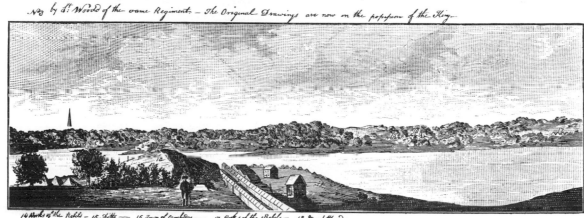

14. Works of the Rebels.   15. Ditto.   16. Town of Cambridge.   17. Works of the Rebels.   18. Mount Whoredom.   70

19. Mount Pisca the strongest post of the Rebels.   20. lines of Encampment of Ditto.   21. Intrenchments of the Rebels.   22. Our lines on Charlestown Heights.   23. Encampment in Ditto.   24. Ruins of Charlestown.   25. R. Boat taken from th__ __   71

THE SIEGE OF BOSTON. FIGS. 68–71: After Lexington and Concord, Boston settled into a state of siege with the colonial militia troops encircling the British-garrisoned city. These four views were sketched by a British officer during that period from Beacon Hill. Dorchester Heights can be seen in FIG. 68. John Hancock's mansion dominates the foreground of FIG. 69. Cambridge can be seen on the far side of the river in FIG. 70. Bunker's and Breed's Hills can be seen to the right of the steeple in FIG. 71.

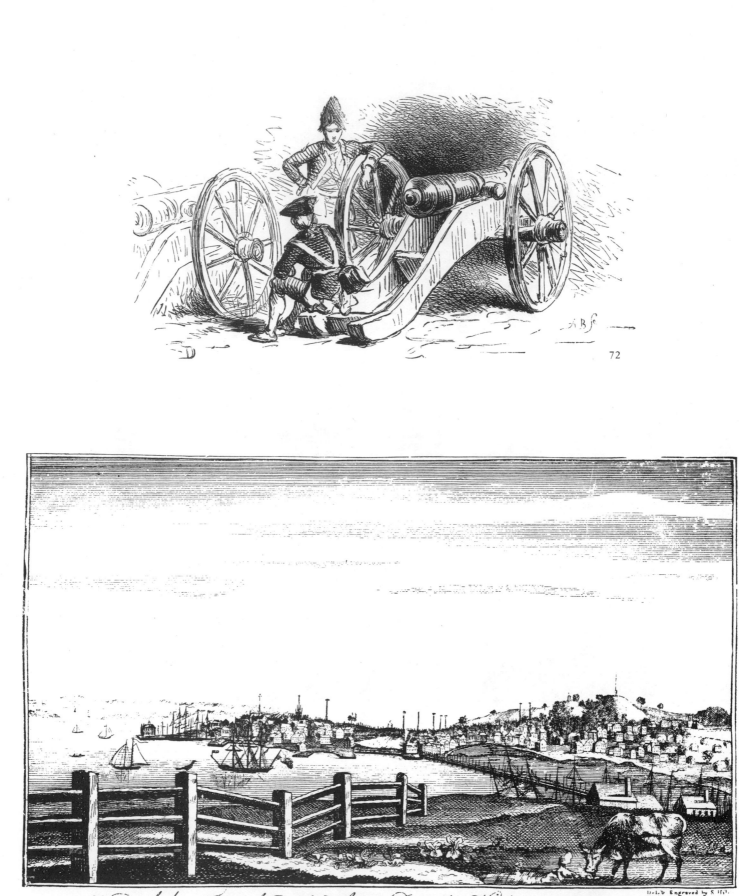

View) of the Town of BOSTON from Breeds Hill in CHARLESTOWN.

72

73

THE SIEGE OF BOSTON (*Continued*). FIG. 72:
British soldiers wait for action beside their artillery. FIG.
73: A contemporary view of Boston from Breed's Hill
in Charlestown.

THE CAPTURE OF FORT TICONDEROGA.
Fig. 74: This engraving after a painting by Alonzo Chappel shows the summons to surrender given by Ethan Allen to Captain De la Place of the Twenty-sixth Cameronians in command of Fort Ticonderoga on Lake Champlain in the early morning of May 10, 1775. The coup by Allen and his Green Mountain Boys was done in conjunction with a force under Benedict Arnold sent by the Provincial Congress of Massachusetts and was carried out with minimal violence. The fort itself was of little military significance, but the British artillery captured with it would later serve the Continental Army well.

ACTION ON BREED'S HILL,
JUNE 17th, 1775.

76

77

THE BATTLE OF BUNKER HILL. Fig. 75: Map of the action at Breed's Hill on Charlestown Peninsula, June 17, 1775. As a move against the entrenched British in Boston, Artemas Ward and the others in command of the American forces outside Boston sent a detail to fortify Bunker Hill on the evening of June 16. By mistake the American troops built their redoubt on Breed's Hill, which is lower, more vulnerable and closer to Boston (Fig. 76). On the morning of the seventeenth the British moved quickly, shelling the Breed's Hill redoubt from ships in the harbor and land batteries and sending a large force of troops across to assault the American position directly. Fig. 77: Prayer before the battle as the British soldiers approached. Fig. 78: Howard Pyle's drawing of colonial militiamen bringing powder to Bunker Hill (*Harper's Magazine,* July, 1886). Fig. 79: The British charge the top of Breed's Hill with bayonets. Fig. 80: The Americans open fire from the redoubt on Breed's Hill. Fig. 81: A British officer looks up the hill toward the American redoubt. Fig. 82: American soldiers and their wounded during a lull in the action.

78

80

79

81

82

83

THE BATTLE OF BUNKER HILL *(Continued)*.
FIG. 83. A Chappel engraving of a scene within the
American lines as one of the British advances closes in.

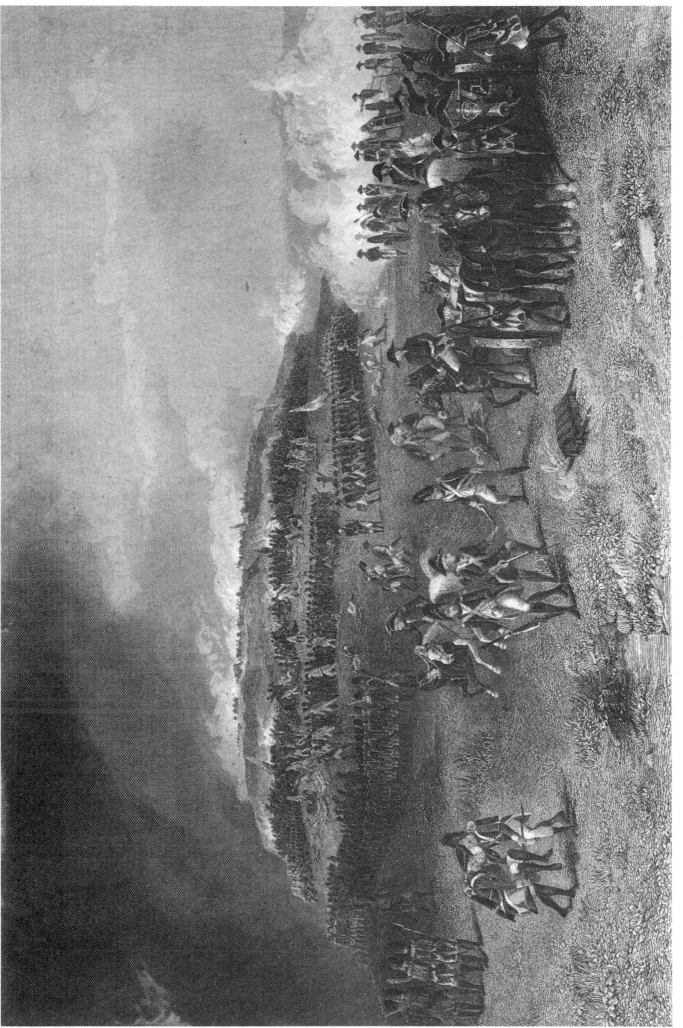

Fig. 84: A Chappel engraving of the British forming up an attack at the base of the hill. The British needed three costly assaults to drive the Americans from Breed's Hill and back to the mainland.

85

THE BATTLE OF BUNKER HILL *(Continued).*
FIG. 85: A panoramic view of Bunker Hill published soon
after the battle. FIG. 86: A mid-nineteenth-century illustration showing ranks of British soldiers moving up the
hill as more artillery is pulled into place below. In both
FIGS. 85 and 86 the effects of the shelling can be seen in
the flames at the top, somewhat enthusiastically rendered.
FIG. 87: A Howard Pyle vignette of British soldiers
marching up the slope of Breed's Hill. Although most of
the fighting took place on Breed's, the battle is always
referred to as Bunker Hill.

87

86

Fig. 88: This 1858 illustration from *Harper's Weekly* shows the intense hand-to-hand combat at the top of the hill. The Americans were finally driven back to the main-land, but records show that the British sustained over a thousand dead and wounded out of the 2,200 men used in the assault, more than twice the casualties sustained by the Americans. The fact that British regular army troops met such fierce resistance from relatively untrained Americans made the battle a moral victory for the colonials.

WASHINGTON TAKING COMMAND. Fig. 89:
The day before the Battle of Bunker Hill, June 16, 1775,
the Second Continental Congress, sitting in Philadelphia,
appointed George Washington Commander-in-Chief of
"the forces raised and to be raised in defence of American
Liberty." These forces of course included the miscellane-
ous group of militia troops which had already formed
themselves into something like an army outside Boston.
This commemorative illustration from *Harper's Weekly*
shows Washington taking command of the army at Cambridge, Massachusetts, after his arrival on July 2. The
artist was C. S. Reinhart.

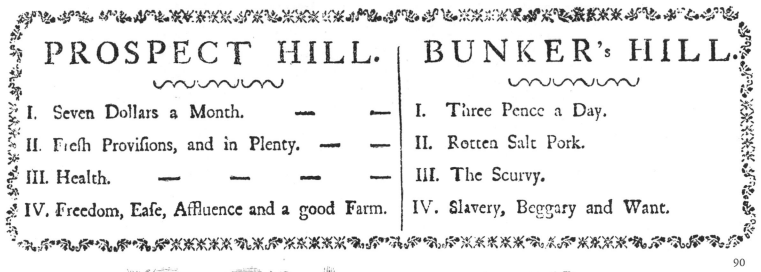

<table>
<tr><td colspan="2">

PROSPECT HILL.

</td><td colspan="2">

BUNKER's HILL.

</td></tr>
</table>

PROSPECT HILL.	BUNKER's HILL.
I. Seven Dollars a Month.	I. Three Pence a Day.
II. Fresh Provisions, and in Plenty.	II. Rotten Salt Pork.
III. Health.	III. The Scurvy.
IV. Freedom, Ease, Affluence and a good Farm.	IV. Slavery, Beggary and Want.

90

91 92

93

94

THE BRITISH EVACUATION OF BOSTON.

FIG. 90: This handbill designed to induce British soldiers to desert was distributed during the winter of 1775–76. FIG. 91: Darley's drawing of Henry Knox's men bringing the British artillery captured at Ticonderoga to Boston. Knox, Boston bookseller turned soldier, and his men brought 59 pieces of ordnance 300 miles through wild country in the dead of winter. On March 5, 1776, the guns were in place on Dorchester Heights overlooking Boston. The British commander, Sir William Howe, had no choice but to abandon Boston, and on March 17 American troops entered the city. FIG. 92: Washington watching the British depart by sea. FIGS. 93–94: Obverse and reverse of medal which Congress awarded to Washington for recapturing Boston, the first such medal ever voted by the American Congress. It was struck after the war and received by Washington in 1786. On the reverse may be seen the artillery on Dorchester Heights overlooking the city.

Two favorite SONGS,

made on the Evacuation of the Town of BOSTON,

by the *Britiſh Troops*, on the 17th of March, 1776.

IN ſeventeen hundred and ſeventy ſix,
  On March the eleventh, the time was prefix'd,
Our forces march'd on upon Dorcheſter-neck,
Made fortifications againſt an attack.
  The morning next following, as Howe did eſpy,
The banks we caſt up, were ſo copious and high,
Said he in three months, all my men with their might,
Cou'd not make two ſuch Forts as they've made in a night.
  Now we hear that their Admiral was very wroth,
And drawing his ſword, he bids Howe to go forth,
And drive off the YANKEES from Dorcheſter hill :
Or he'd leave the harbour and him to their will.
  Howe rallies his forces upon the next day,

IT was'nt our will that Bunker Hill
  From us ſhould e,er be taken :
We thought 'twould never be retook,
  But we find we are Miſtaken.

The ſoldiers bid the hill farewell,
  Two images left ſentreis,
This they had done all out of fun
  To the American Yankees.

A flag of truce was ſent thereon,
  To ſee if the hill was clear,
No living ſoul was found thereon,
  But theſe images ſtood there.

95

96

THE EVACUATION OF BOSTON *(Continued)*.
FIG. 95: A contemporary broadside celebrates the recapture of the city by the colonials. FIG. 96: Engraving of a painting by M. A. Wageman shows the British boarding ships to leave Boston. Cannon barrels are being dumped off a wharf to prevent capture.

97

THE ATTACK ON FORT MOULTRIE. FIG. 97:
The South's leading port, Charleston, as it appeared in
1780. The British attempt to take Charleston in June,
1776, with a fleet under Admiral Sir Peter Parker became the Southern equivalent of Bunker Hill, with the
difference that here the colonials achieved a military as
well as a moral victory. FIG. 98: Citizens of Charleston
crowning an effigy symbolizing liberty. FIG. 99: The
British launched their attack on the American fort on
Sullivan's Island, guarding the channel into Charleston's
harbor, on June 28, 1776. This illustration shows the first
British ships closing in on the fort. The Stars and Stripes
flag in the center is an anachronism; the actual flag flown
at Sullivan's Island had the half-moon design shown in
FIGS. 100 and 102.

98

99

THE ATTACK ON FORT MOULTRIE *(Continued)*. FIGS. 100–102: Three illustrations of one of the legendary figures of the Revolution, Sergeant Jasper, protecting the flag on Sullivan's Island. FIG. 101 reproduces Howard Pyle's drawing of Sergeant Jasper from *Harper's Magazine,* October, 1883.

100

101

102

Fig. 103: This 1858 illustration from *Harper's Weekly* shows the Americans at Sullivan's Island firing on the British fleet. The sand and palmetto-log fort absorbed the British shelling while Parker's ships took a terrible pounding and ultimately withdrew. Celebrating this great victory, the Americans named the fort on Sullivan's Island for its commander William Moultrie.

104

109

105

110

106

107

108

THE DECLARATION OF INDEPENDENCE.

FIGS. 104–105: Two views of the Pennsylvania State House, later named Independence Hall, where the Continental Congress turned to the question of declaring independence from Great Britain in the spring and summer of 1776. FIG. 106: Ringing the Liberty Bell on July 4, 1776. FIG. 107: Seal used by Jefferson bearing his monogram and the inscription "Rebellion to tyrants is obedience to God." FIG. 108: The Liberty Bell. FIG. 109: Monticello, Virginia, home of Thomas Jefferson, author of the Declaration of Independence. FIG. 110: The house in Philadelphia where Jefferson stayed while writing the Declaration.

111

113

112

114

FIG. 111: Thomas Jefferson, after a print by Desnoyers. Largely at the suggestion of John Adams, Jefferson was the member of the Committee of Congress charged with the task of preparing the Declaration who was selected to do the actual writing. FIG. 112: Jefferson, from an engraving done while he was in Paris. FIG. 113: John Adams, from a portrait by Gilbert Stuart. Adams was the most effective debater in the Congress as he urged adoption of Jefferson's Declaration. FIG. 114: Richard Henry Lee, from a portrait by Alonzo Chappel. On June 7, 1776, Lee introduced in Congress the fateful resolution calling for independence from England.

DECLARATION OF INDEPENDENCE.

In Congress 4th July, 1776.

ORIGINAL DRAFT OF THE DECLARATION OF INDEPENDENCE. Fig. 115: Jefferson preserved his original draft of the Declaration of Independence, reproduced here in its entirety.

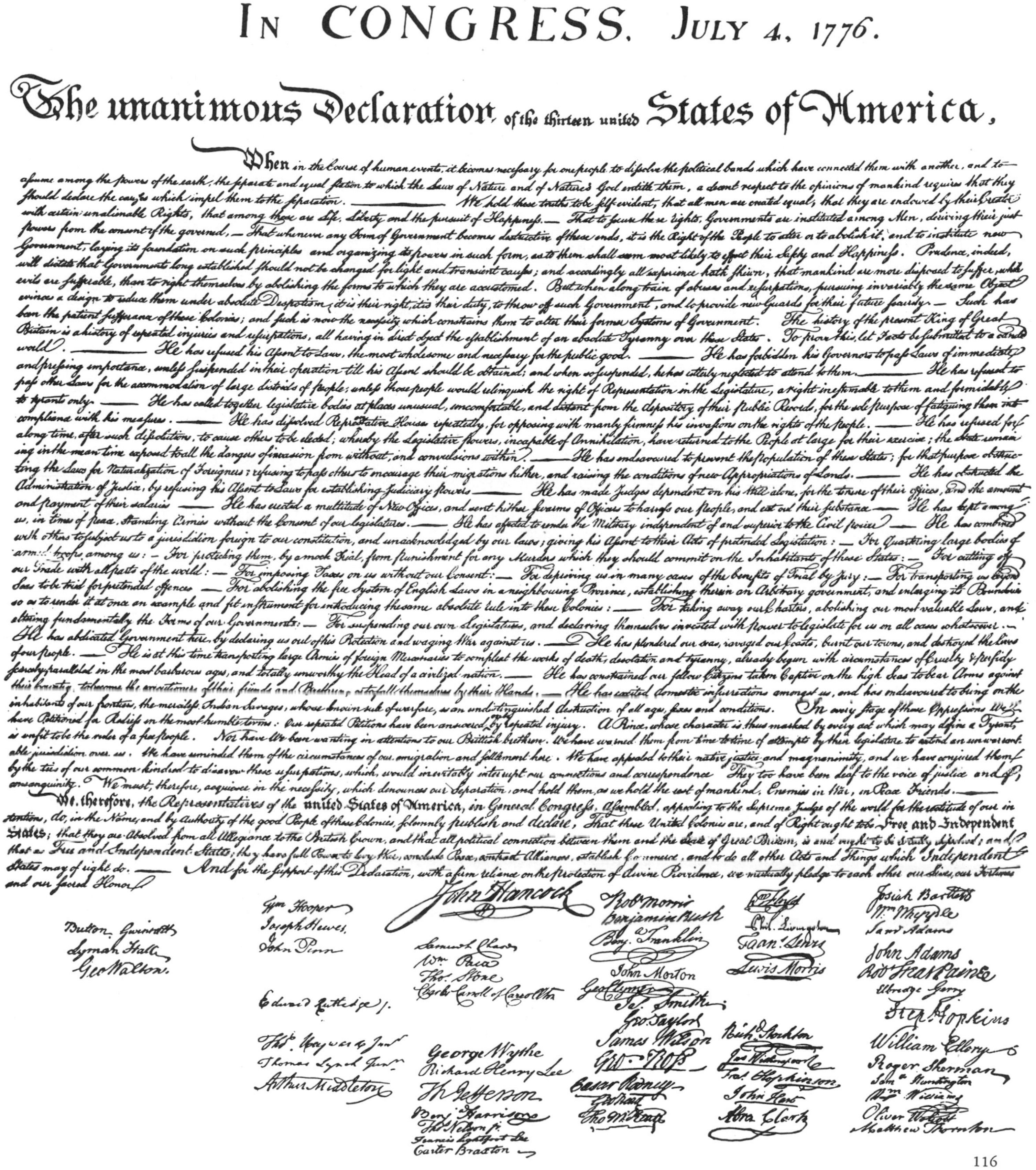

THE DECLARATION OF INDEPENDENCE.
FIG. 116: Congress passed the resolution calling for independence on July 2, 1776. On July 4, the formal Declaration was adopted. This illustration reproduces the formal Declaration engrossed on parchment, probably by Timothy Matlack of Philadelphia, and signed by most members of Congress on August 2, 1776.

In CONGRESS, July 4, 1776.

A DECLARATION

By the REPRESENTATIVES of the

UNITED STATES OF AMERICA,

In GENERAL CONGRESS ASSEMBLED.

WHEN in the Courſe of human Events, It becomes neceſſary for one People to diſſolve the Political Bands which have connected them with another, and to aſſume among the Powers of the Earth, the ſeparate and equal Station to which the Laws of Nature and of Nature's God entitle them, a decent Reſpect to the Opinions of Mankind requires that they ſhould declare the cauſes which impel them to the Separation.

We hold theſe Truths to be ſelf-evident, that all Men are created equal, that they are endowed by their Creator with certain unalienable Rights, that among theſe are Life, Liberty, and the Purſuit of Happineſs—That to ſecure theſe Rights, Governments are inſtituted among Men, deriving their juſt Powers from the Conſent of the Governed, that whenever any Form of Government becomes deſtructive of theſe Ends, it is the Right of the People to alter or to aboliſh it, and to inſtitute new Government, laying its Foundation on ſuch Principles, and organizing its Powers in ſuch Form, as to them ſhall ſeem moſt likely to effect their Safety and Happineſs. Prudence, indeed, will dictate that Governments long eſtabliſhed ſhould not be changed for light and tranſient Cauſes; and accordingly all Experience hath ſhewn, that Mankind are more diſpoſed to ſuffer, while Evils are ſufferable, than to right themſelves by aboliſhing the Forms to which they are accuſtomed. But when a long Train of Abuſes and Uſurpations, purſuing invariably the ſame Object, evinces a Deſign to reduce them under abſolute Deſpotiſm, it is their Right, it is their Duty, to throw off ſuch Government, and to provide new Guards for their future Security. Such has been the patient Sufferance of theſe Colonies; and ſuch is now the Neceſſity which conſtrains them to alter their former Syſtems of Government. The Hiſtory of the preſent King of Great-Britain is a Hiſtory of repeated Injuries and Uſurpations, all having in direct Object the Eſtabliſhment of an abſolute Tyranny over theſe States. To prove this, let Facts be ſubmitted to a candid World.

He has refuſed his Aſſent to Laws, the moſt wholeſome and neceſſary for the public Good.

He has forbidden his Governors to paſs Laws of immediate and preſſing Importance, unleſs ſuſpended in their Operation till his Aſſent ſhould be obtained; and when ſo ſuſpended, he has utterly neglected to attend to them.

He has refuſed to paſs other Laws for the Accommodation of large Diſtricts of People, unleſs thoſe People would relinquiſh the Right of Repreſentation in the Legiſlature, a Right ineſtimable to them, and formidable to Tyrants only.

He has called together Legiſlative Bodies at Places unuſual, uncomfortable, and diſtant from the Depoſitory of their public Records, for the ſole Purpoſe of fatiguing them into Compliance with his Meaſures.

He has diſſolved Repreſentative Houſes repeatedly, for oppoſing with manly Firmneſs his Invaſions on the Rights of the People.

He has refuſed for a long Time, after ſuch Diſſolutions, to cauſe others to be elected; whereby the Legiſlative Powers, incapable of Annihilation, have returned to the People at large for their exerciſe; the State remaining in the mean time expoſed to all the Dangers of Invaſion from without, and Convulſions within.

He has endeavoured to prevent the Population of theſe States; for that Purpoſe obſtructing the Laws for Naturalization of Foreigners; refuſing to paſs others to encourage their Migrations hither, and raiſing the Conditions of new Appropriations of Lands.

He has obſtructed the Adminiſtration of Juſtice, by refuſing his Aſſent to Laws for eſtabliſhing Judiciary Powers.

He has made Judges dependent on his Will alone, for the Tenure of their Offices, and the Amount and Payment of their Salaries.

He has erected a Multitude of new Offices, and ſent hither Swarms of Officers to harraſs our People, and eat out their Subſtance.

He has kept among us, in Times of Peace, Standing Armies, without the conſent of our Legiſlatures.

He has affected to render the Military independent of and ſuperior to the Civil Power.

He has combined with others to ſubject us to a Juriſdiction foreign to our Conſtitution, and unacknowledged by our Laws; giving his Aſſent to their Acts of pretended Legiſlation:

For quartering large Bodies of Armed Troops among us:

For protecting them, by a mock Trial, from Puniſhment for any Murders which they ſhould commit on the Inhabitants of theſe States:

For cutting off our Trade with all Parts of the World:

For impoſing Taxes on us without our Conſent:

For depriving us, in many Caſes, of the Benefits of Trial by Jury:

For tranſporting us beyond Seas to be tried for pretended Offences:

For aboliſhing the free Syſtem of Engliſh Laws in a neighbouring Province, eſtabliſhing therein an arbitrary Government, and enlarging its Boundaries, ſo as to render it at once an Example and fit Inſtrument for introducing the ſame abſolute Rule into theſe Colonies:

For taking away our Charters, aboliſhing our moſt valuable Laws, and altering fundamentally the Forms of our Governments:

For ſuſpending our own Legiſlatures, and declaring themſelves inveſted with Power to legiſlate for us in all Caſes whatſoever.

He has abdicated Government here, by declaring us out of his Protection and waging War againſt us.

He has plundered our Seas, ravaged our Coaſts, burnt our Towns, and deſtroyed the Lives of our People.

He is, at this Time, tranſporting large Armies of foreign Mercenaries to compleat the Works of Death, Deſolation, and Tyranny, already begun with circumſtances of Cruelty and Perfidy, ſcarcely paralleled in the moſt barbarous Ages, and totally unworthy the Head of a civilized Nation.

He has conſtrained our fellow Citizens taken Captive on the high Seas to bear Arms againſt their Country, to become the Executioners of their Friends and Brethren, or to fall themſelves by their Hands.

He has excited domeſtic Inſurrections amongſt us, and has endeavoured to bring on the Inhabitants of our Frontiers, the mercileſs Indian Savages, whoſe known Rule of Warfare, is an undiſtinguiſhed Deſtruction, of all Ages, Sexes and Conditions.

In every ſtage of theſe Oppreſſions we have Petitioned for Redreſs in the moſt humble Terms: Our repeated Petitions have been anſwered only by repeated Injury. A Prince, whoſe Character is thus marked by every act which may define a Tyrant, is unfit to be the Ruler of a free People.

Nor have we been wanting in Attentions to our Britiſh Brethren. We have warned them from Time to Time of Attempts by their Legiſlature to extend an unwarrantable Juriſdiction over us. We have reminded them of the Circumſtances of our Emigration and Settlement here. We have appealed to their native Juſtice and Magnanimity, and we have conjured them by the Ties of our common Kindred to diſavow theſe Uſurpations, which would inevitably interrupt our Connections and Correſpondence. They too have been deaf to the Voice of Juſtice and of Conſanguinity. We muſt, therefore, acquieſce in the Neceſſity, which denounces our Separation, and hold them, as we hold the reſt of Mankind, Enemies in War, in Peace, Friends.

We, therefore, the Repreſentatives of the UNITED STATES OF AMERICA, in GENERAL CONGRESS, Aſſembled, appealing to the Supreme Judge of the World for the Rectitude of our Intentions, do, in the Name, and by Authority of the good People of theſe Colonies, ſolemnly Publiſh and Declare, That theſe United Colonies are, and of Right ought to be, FREE AND INDEPENDENT STATES; that they are abſolved from all Allegiance to the Britiſh Crown, and that all political Connection between them and the State of Great-Britain, is and ought to be totally diſſolved; and that as FREE AND INDEPENDENT STATES, they have full Power to levy War, conclude Peace, contract Alliances, eſtabliſh Commerce, and to do all other Acts and Things which INDEPENDENT STATES may of right do. And for the ſupport of this Declaration, with a firm Reliance on the Protection of divine Providence, we mutually pledge to each other our Lives, our Fortunes, and our ſacred Honor.

Signed by ORDER and in BEHALF of the CONGRESS,

JOHN HANCOCK, President.

ATTEST.
CHARLES THOMSON, Secretary.

PHILADELPHIA: PRINTED BY JOHN DUNLAP.

117

THE DECLARATION OF INDEPENDENCE (Continued). Fig. 117: Reproduction of the Declaration as printed by order of Congress by John Dunlap of Philadelphia.

FIG. 118: Engraving after John Trumbull's well-known painting often titled "The Signing of the Declaration of Independence." Actually, the painting portrays the presentation of the Declaration to the Congress by the committee which prepared it. As is well known, it is a kind of composite portrait, painted throughout a period of years after the event; not all the members of Congress portrayed in it were all present on July 2, July 4, or August 2, when most of the members signed.

THE DECLARATION OF INDEPENDENCE
(Continued). FIG. 119: Commemorative plate issued by the Department of State in 1819; the signature of John Quincy Adams vouches for the authenticity of the copies of the signatures of the Declaration's signers reproduced on it. The names are surrounded by a border comprised of the State Seals of the original Thirteen States and a view of the Capitol Building in Washington.

THE FIRST PUBLIC READING OF THE DECLARATION. Fig. 120: Howard Pyle drew this illustration of the members of Congress leaving Independence Hall on the occasion of the first public reading of the Declaration on July 8, 1776. Many members of Congress are identifiable, and the dense crowd lends the composition a feeling of serious common purpose. One member may be seen carrying away a copy of the first printed version. *Harper's Weekly*, July, 1880.

THE FIRST PUBLIC READING OF THE
DECLARATION (*Continued*). FIG. 121: On July 15,
1876, *Harper's Weekly* published this illustration by
Edwin A. Abbey of John Nixon giving the first public
reading from the steps of Independence Hall. Nixon was
a member of the Philadelphia Committee of Safety in the
period before the Revolution. Similar public readings followed throughout the colonies as the Declaration was
circulated.

121

THE DECLARATION OF INDEPENDENCE.
FIGS. 122–126: Five Howard Pyle drawings of public
readings of the Declaration of Independence during the
summer of 1776 — at Boston; Williamsburg; Charleston; Portsmouth, New Hampshire; and Newport.

51

127

THE DECLARATION OF INDEPENDENCE
(Continued). FIG. 127: The Declaration being read to
Washington's army in New York, July 9, 1776, as drawn
by Howard Pyle for *Harper's Magazine,* July, 1892.

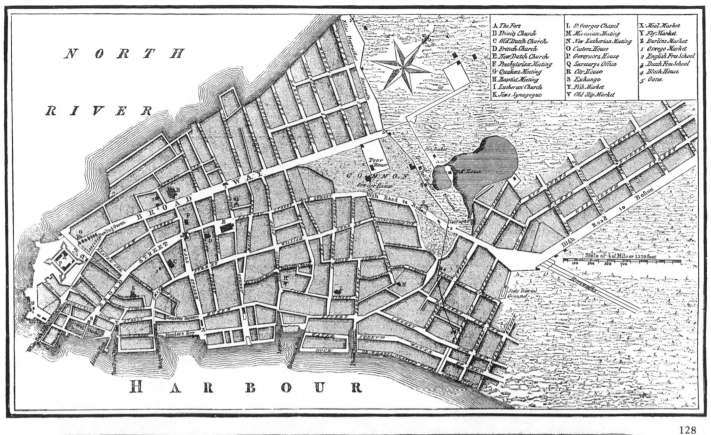

128

129

NEW YORK AND THE AMERICAN REVOLU-
TION. FIG. 128: This 1767 map of New York represents what is now only the very lowest portion of Manhattan. FIG. 129: A view of New York in 1776 from
the west bank of the Hudson River. Violent opposition
to England's taxation policies in the years before the
Revolution centered in Boston, and New York was
throughout the Revolution a stronghold of Tory senti-
ment; New York's Sons of Liberty, however, had their
moments. FIG. 130: Darley's drawing of New Yorkers
defending their Liberty Pole; similar poles or, more often,
trees were used in many places to mark the meeting spots
of the Sons of Liberty and other similar groups.

130

131

132

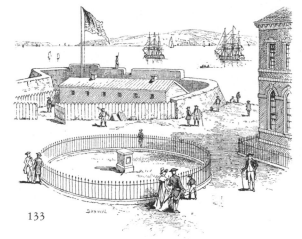

133

135

134

NEW YORK AND THE AMERICAN REVOLU-
TION *(Continued)*. FIG. 131: New Yorkers protesting
the Stamp Act of 1765. FIG. 132: New Yorkers receiving
news of the action at Lexington and Concord. FIG. 133:
New York's Bowling Green before the Revolution. On
July 9, 1776, after Washington's army had reached New
York from Boston and the Declaration of Independence
had been read to the troops, the event was followed by a
bonfire (FIG. 134) and the tearing down of the eques-
trian statue of George III (FIG. 135). The statue was
later melted down into bullets for the American army.

136

137

FIG. 136: This contemporary cut was evidently meant to
illustrate the same scene as FIG. 135, but was executed
by a patriot artist who had apparently never seen the
statue. FIG. 137: Howard Pyle's illustration from *Harper's Weekly* of December 25, 1880, shows a New York
street scene just before the Revolution.

THE BATTLE OF LONG ISLAND. Fig. 138: This engraving of a painting by Alonzo Chappel shows the Americans under William Alexander (the self-styled Lord Stirling) retreating across Gowanus Creek on August 27, 1776, in the face of a heavy British onslaught. The British landed with 32,000 English and Hessian troops, the largest expeditionary force in England's history up to that time, and the result was a complete American rout. The Americans suffered over a thousand casualties on that day, and only Stirling's ably directed rear-guard action prevented total disaster.

139

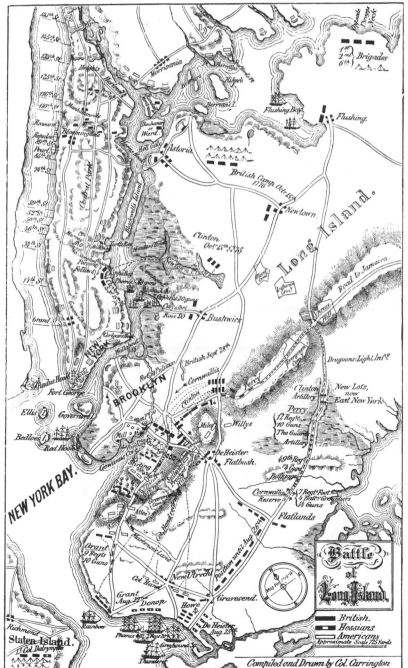

140

141

FIG. 139: The Americans limped back to Brooklyn Heights from where, on the night of August 29, John Glover's Marblehead mariners ferried the entire American army of 9,500 men across to Manhattan under cover of rain and fog (FIG. 140). The figure on horseback is no doubt meant to represent Washington, who personally directed the retreat. It is doubtful that the Americans ever came quite so close to losing the war at one stroke. The Battle of Long Island was followed by other disasters near Manhattan, such as the action at Fort Washington on November 15 (FIG. 141). FIG. 142: Map of the Battle of Long Island and subsequent action, published in 1876.

142

THE RETREAT FROM BROOKLYN HEIGHTS.
FIG. 143: Washington directing the retreat from Brooklyn Heights to New York. British officers were later to state that the successful carrying out of this massive retreat under desperate conditions and in so short a time had to be considered one of the most remarkable achievements in the history of warfare.

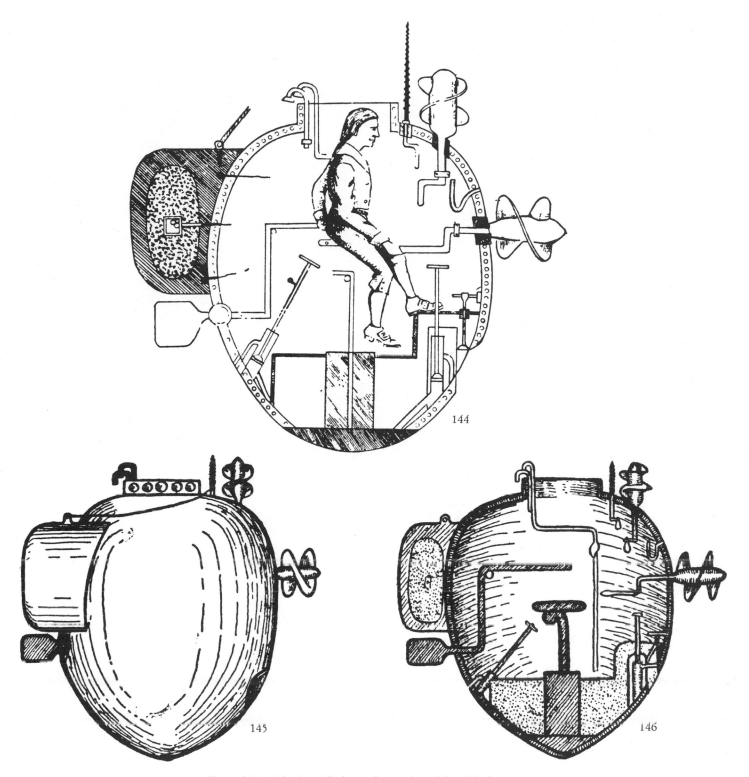

144

145 146

FIGS. 144–146: A sidelight to the battle of New York was the exploit of the world's first combat submarine, named, appropriately enough, "The Turtle," and built by David Bushnell of Saybrook, Connecticut.. FIG. 144: A diagram showing the position of the operator of "The Turtle." The submarine had enough air to support life for half an hour; a bottle of phosphorus was used to illuminate the compass and water gauge — water was admitted into the bottom to submerge the submarine and then pumped out for surfacing. On September 6, 1776, "The Turtle" approached the flagship of the British fleet. However, the copper-sheathed hull of H.M.S. "Eagle" was too tough for the bomb carried by the submarine to be attached securely. The subsequent explosion did no damage either to the ship or "The Turtle's" operator, an army sergeant named Ezra Lee, but it did give the British Admiral Howe an unwelcome scare.

NATHAN HALE. Fig. 147: The execution of Nathan Hale as conceived by Darley.

148

FIG. 148: The same scene as illustrated in *Harper's Weekly* in October, 1880. On September 21, 1776, Hale, formerly a member of a Connecticut regiment who served in the siege of Boston, was captured within British lines in New York in the disguise of a Dutch schoolteacher. He did not deny being a spy and, in accordance with military law, was hanged the next day near present-day Sixty-third Street and First Avenue. Modern research has indicated that Hale probably never said "I only regret that I have but one life to lose for my country," but remarked instead only on the necessity for soldiers to obey orders. FIG. 149: Howard Pyle's drawing of the hanging of Hale (from *Harper's Magazine,* June, 1880). As no authentic portrait of Hale exists, it will readily be seen that all these artists were improvising when it came to capturing the appearance of their hero.

149

WASHINGTON CROSSING THE DELAWARE.
Fig. 150: One of the most famous pictorial images produced by the American Revolution, Washington crossing
the Delaware, in an engraving after the painting by
Emanuel Leutze. The historical inaccuracies in Leutze's
painting have often been discussed; the boat shown is the
wrong size and shape, the flag being carried was not in
use until six months later, and Washington himself is
portrayed in a posture that would likely have resulted in
his drowning on that stormy night. Despite these faults,
the painting, executed in 1851 in Düsseldorf, has endured
as a kind of monument to the spirit of the occasion.

151

152

153

FIGS. 151 and 153: Two more views of the crossing of the Delaware. On Christmas Night, 1776, Washington crossed the river with 2,400 men and eighteen pieces of artillery and won a devastating victory over the Hessian garrison at Trenton early the next day. It was a consummate tactical victory, relying heavily on the element of surprise, and provided the American army with a badly needed psychological lift after the series of defeats that had begun on Long Island in the summer and culminated in the retreat through New Jersey. FIG. 152: This Barber woodcut portrays the kind of ore barge used on that night, although even here everyone on board appears to be standing. FIG. 154: A mid-nineteenth-century engraving of the crossing that owes many of its details to paintings of the scene by both Edward Hicks and Thomas Sully. The central figure on horseback is of course Washington.

154

155

156

157

158

THE BATTLE OF TRENTON. Figs. 155–157: Three views by H. A. Ogden of the action at Trenton: crossing the Delaware, marching to Trenton, and Washington's directing of the artillery. Fig. 158: Washington's visit to the mortally wounded Hessian commander Johann Rall. In addition to Rall, over a thousand Hessians were killed or captured at Trenton; the American army sustained only four wounded — a total victory.

159

160

161

Fig. 159: An engraving after Trumbull's painting of the American victory at Princeton. Fig. 160: From Trenton the action shifted to Princeton on January 3, 1777. After some tactical maneuvers against the British commander Cornwallis, which almost resulted in another disaster for his army, Washington outflanked the British and won a victory against their rear guard. Darley portrayed Washington directing his troops. Fig. 161: After Princeton the American army went into winter quarters at Morristown, New Jersey. This Barber woodcut depicts the scene. Fig. 162: Washington's headquarters during the winter at Morristown.

162

163

164

165

166

167

168

THE BATTLE OF THE BRANDYWINE. Fig.

163: American forces at the battle of Brandywine Creek. In the late summer of 1777, the British Commander Howe landed with his army from New York at the northern tip of Chesapeake Bay, fifty miles from his objective, Philadelphia. Washington met Howe at the Brandywine on September 11 and suffered a tactical defeat largely through insufficient knowledge of the terrain. Later that month the British army occupied Philadelphia, driving the American Congress first to Lancaster and then to York. Washington attacked the British at their main base, Germantown, on October 4, and nearly won a major victory before being forced back. Figs. 164 and 166: Two views of the American attack on the house of Benjamin Chew, a British stronghold at Germantown. The time and effort spent trying to take the British-fortified mansion probably cost Washington his chance of victory. Fig. 165: British soldiers attacking Fort Mercer in November. By taking Fort Mercer, near present-day Red Bank, and nearby Fort Mifflin, the British solidified their hold on the area. Washington withdrew to Valley Forge, and arrived there December 19.

169

THE BATTLE OF ORISKANY. Figs. 167–169:
While Howe and Washington were engaged around Philadelphia in the late summer and fall of 1777, the major action of the year, as seen from our present perspective, was taking place in upper New York State in the action which culminated in the turning point of Saratoga. The British plan has often been discussed: Burgoyne was to drive south from Canada and join forces with Col. Barry St. Leger, who was driving east through the Mohawk Valley to meet him. Meanwhile, Howe was to come up from New York, and their combined forces would cut New England off from the rest of the erstwhile colonies and prepare for a coordinated major strike at Washington's army. As we have seen, Howe sailed for Philadelphia before receiving his orders to advance north, leaving Burgoyne and St. Leger on their own. St. Leger

found his route blocked by American forces at Fort Stanwix on the Mohawk. American Brig. Gen. Nicholas Herkimer came north with 800 men to help hold Stanwix. Herkimer's men were ambushed by the British and their Indian allies at Oriskany on August 6, 1777. Herkimer was mortally wounded, and his men retreated; but the bloody battle left the British and Indians in little better shape. Two weeks later, his mission not accomplished, St. Leger, his Indian support scared off by rumors of the great American force massing in the area, broke off the siege of Stanwix and headed back for Oswego, leaving Burgoyne without support. Fig. 167: The Oriskany battlefield as later sketched by Benson Lossing. Fig. 168: A Barber woodcut of the wounded Herkimer, still directing his troops. Fig. 169: The wounded Herkimer at Oriskany.

THE BATTLE OF ORISKANY (*Continued*). FIG. 170: This 1857 illustration from *Ballou's Pictorial* shows the fierce hand-to-hand combat at Oriskany.

THE BATTLE OF BENNINGTON. FIG. 171: Alonzo Chappel's painting of the Battle of Bennington, August 16, 1777. General John Stark, commander of the New Hampshire army, is on horseback in the right center directing his men. The loss of 800 Hessians in the total American victory at Bennington, in present-day southern Vermont, was another disaster that fell to Burgoyne en route to Saratoga. FIG. 172: Chappel's painting of Stark. Stark had left Washington's army after the Battle of Trenton, feeling that Congress had not recognized his merit. He had agreed to command the force at Bennington only because it was an army raised solely by the state of New Hampshire and was not connected with the Continentals.

172

173

174

175

176

177

178

SARATOGA. Fig. 173: General John Burgoyne. Fig. 174: Burgoyne meeting with his Indian allies at Saratoga. Burgoyne went to great lengths—largely without success— to prevent the Indians from committing atrocities upon the civilian population on his way to Saratoga. After the disaster at Bennington, most of the Indians deserted him and went back to Canada, leaving the British general without these effective and capable scouts. Fig. 175: Barber's woodcut of the funeral of British General Simon Fraser, killed by an American sharpshooter at Saratoga. The engagement known as the Battle of Saratoga was actually two major battles. The first, on September 19, 1777, at Freeman's Farm, saw an attempted British breakthrough turned into a critical American victory, largely through the efforts of Daniel Morgan and his riflemen. Fig. 176: Trumbull's portrait of Morgan (in characteristic uniform) engraved by J. F. E. Prud'homme. Morgan retired from the army in 1779, but came back to deliver an equally brilliant performance in the South at the Cowpens in 1781. Fig. 177: Engraving after Trumbull's portrait of General Philip Schuyler, the American area-commander in upper New York State. Schuyler had been instrumental in impeding Burgoyne's progress toward Saratoga. Figs. 178–179: The Second Battle of Freeman's Farm was fought on October 7, 1777; when it was over, Burgoyne's army was finished, and with

179

it British hopes for a quick end to the war. Fig. 178: The wounded figure of Benedict Arnold dominates the center of this illustration of the American attack on a Hessian redoubt. While Horatio Gates was nominally in charge of the American forces at Saratoga, and claimed credit for the victory, real credit has to go to Stark, Morgan, and Arnold, who was brilliant in the last battle he fought on the American side. Fig. 179: A mid-nineteenth-century illustration of the action at Saratoga.

THE SURRENDER AT SARATOGA. Fig. 180: A French engraving, somewhat idealized, of Burgoyne surrendering to Gates on October 17, 1777.

180

Fig. 181: Engraving after John Trumbull's painting of Burgoyne's surrender. Burgoyne is offering his sword to Gates. Daniel Morgan is at Gates' side, in white, and Philip Schuyler may be seen at the extreme right, not in uniform. The surrender of a British and German army of 5,000 men at Saratoga has always been considered the turning point of the war, although Yorktown was still four long years away. The American victory had one effect that was immediately measurable, however; it convinced the French that an American alliance could be worthwhile. Within four months the treaty pledging military support for the United States was signed. If Saratoga is today seen as the turning point, that is the reason.

BENJAMIN FRANKLIN IN PARIS. FIG. 182: Illustration by John Andrew from *Ballou's Pictorial*, May 17, 1856, showing Benjamin Franklin being presented at the French court. Franklin's diplomatic efforts paid off on February 6, 1778, when the long-negotiated treaty with France was signed.

183

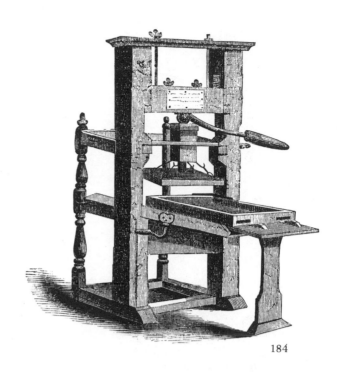

184

Fig. 183: Engraving of a portrait of Franklin from a painting by Duplessis. Fig. 184: A printing press of the type used by Franklin as a Philadelphia printer and publisher. Fig. 185: Engraving of a portrait of Franklin.

185

186

187

188

189

191

190

VALLEY FORGE. FIG. 186: Darley's drawing of the American army marching to Valley Forge, 20 miles northwest of Philadelphia, where the 11,000-man force spent the winter of 1777–78. The spot took its name from an abandoned iron forge. FIG. 187: The army in camp at Valley Forge. FIG. 188: Another view by Darley of the march to Valley Forge. FIG. 189: Only after his army had moved from canvas tents into their huts did Washington occupy this house as his headquarters. FIG. 190: With the winter too cold to be withstood in tents, the American soldiers built a virtual city out of log huts. FIG. 191: The army at Valley Forge. FIG. 192: Washington requisitioned supplies from the neighborhood with proclamations such as this. These efforts met with only erratic success.

By His EXCELLENCY

GEORGE WASHINGTON, Esquire,

GENERAL and COMMANDER in CHIEF of the Forces of the UNITED STATES OF AMERICA.

BY Virtue of the Power and Direction to Me especially given, I hereby enjoin and require all Persons residing within seventy Miles of my Head Quarters to thresh one Half of their Grain by the 1st Day of February, and the other Half by the 1st Day of March next ensuing, on Pain, in Case of Failure of having all that shall remain in Sheaves after the Period above mentioned, seized by the Commissaries and Quarter-Masters of the Army, and paid for as Straw

GIVEN under my Hand, at Head Quarters, near the Valley Forge, in Philadelphia County, this 20th Day of December, 1777.

G. WASHINGTON.

By His Excellency's Command,

ROBERT H. HARRISON, Sec'y.

LANCASTER: PRINTED BY JOHN DUNLAP.

192

VALLEY FORGE (*Continued*). FIG. 193: A scene at Valley Forge, showing some of the completed huts. The figure on horseback is no doubt meant to represent Washington. FIG. 194: An American soldier at Valley Forge. The tattered uniform and absence of boots accurately reflect the conditions under which the army survived. FIG. 195: Baron Frederick William Augustus von Steuben. Steuben was a former Prussian army officer who met Franklin in Paris. Franklin sent him to Washington at Valley Forge, where he promptly began drilling the American army into a far more organized and sophisticated fighting force than it had ever been.

197

196

FIG. 196: Darley's drawing of Steuben drilling troops at
Valley Forge. FIG. 197: A Barber woodcut of Steuben
and American troops. FIG. 198: Chappel's painting of
Steuben on horseback.

198

VALLEY FORGE *(Continued)*. FIG. 199: A page of
drawings by C. S. Reinhart illustrating scenes at Valley
Forge. Washington ponders his problems as his army
simply endures. If there was a bright moment at Valley
Forge it must have been when news arrived of the French
alliance, signed while the army was in camp there.

Fig. 200: Washington reviewing the troops at Valley Forge in an illustration by John Andrew which was published in *Eallou's Pictorial* on September 13, 1856.

VALLEY FORGE (*Continued*). FIG. 201: Life at Valley Forge as pictured by Julian Scott for *Harper's Weekly* in 1877. This view shows a wagon carrying logs for the soldiers' huts with a sentry on duty at right.

202

THE BATTLE OF MONMOUTH COURT HOUSE. Fig. 202: Washington rallying the American army at Monmouth. In late June, 1778, Sir Henry Clinton, British commander in Philadelphia, received orders to evacuate that city and return with his army to New York. Fearing to go by sea because of the possibility that a French fleet, now that the alliance had been signed, might appear at any time off America, Clinton decided to march his main army overland through New Jersey to Sandy Hook, from where he could easily cross to New York. The plan provided Washington, still at Valley Forge, with a golden opportunity to strike a major blow at the enemy's army, strung out in a long line of march. Unfortunately, protocol demanded that command of the attacking American force had to go to General Charles Lee, the one senior American officer who was convinced that the Americans could not win a direct confrontation with the British. Lee's forces met the British at Monmouth Court House (now Freehold) on June 28. With a display of incompetence the proportions of which still amaze military historians, Lee attacked timidly, then inexplicably ordered a general retreat, leaving Anthony Wayne and other subordinate commanders stranded in forward posi-

203

tions without support. The effect was to cost Washington's army its chance for a major crushing victory. By the time Washington rushed up from the rear, fired Lee, and tried to rally the American forces, it was too late to achieve anything but a draw. Fig. 203: Washington rushing to the front to relieve Lee of his command, as drawn by H. A. Ogden.

205

206

THE BATTLE OF MONMOUTH COURT
HOUSE *(Continued)*. FIG. 204: The legendary Molly
Pitcher who during the battle took over the cannon which
had been manned by her fallen husband. FIG. 205: The
field at Monmouth from a sketch by Lossing after a
painting by George Washington Parke Custis, a descen-
dant of Martha Washington. FIG. 206: A contemporary
caricature of the irascible Lee which acquaintances said
was actually a remarkably good likeness. FIG. 207: Darley's sketch of the scene at Monmouth.

207

THE BATTLE OF MONMOUTH COURT HOUSE *(Continued)*. Fig. 208: An 1858 illustration from *Harper's Weekly* showing Washington taking over from Lee at Monmouth. Lee was court-martialed and his participation in the war ended. After the near miss at Monmouth the British and American armies were never to meet again in a major action in the North. The British settled in New York while Washington encamped at White Plains and the focus of the conflict shifted to the South.

209

STONY POINT. Fɪɢ. 209: The storming of Stony
Point. While there was no major action in the North after
Monmouth, there was activity. One episode occurred at
Stony Point on the Hudson, 35 miles above New York.
The British always wanted command of the Hudson, even
after Burgoyne's disaster in 1777. On May 30, 1779,
Clinton sent 6,000 men up the Hudson from New York
and took two American forts, the one at Stony Point and
another at Verplanck's Point. On July 15 the Americans
retaliated; Washington sent Anthony Wayne with 1,300
troops, who recaptured Stony Point after a brutal bayonet
fight. Fɪɢ. 210: Another view of the storming of Stony
Point.

210

211

212

213

STONY POINT (*Continued*). FIG. 211: "Mad" Anthony Wayne, nicknamed by a deserter's complaint, after a painting by Chappel. FIG. 212: Obverse and reverse of medal which Congress awarded to Wayne. Soon after the battle Washington decided that Stony Point could well become too difficult to maintain and ordered it abandoned, but Wayne's adventure discouraged any further British offensive moves up the river. The British command came to realize there was only one way they could win *the* major objective on the Hudson, West Point, and that was by quite a different method. FIG. 213: Darley's drawing of Wayne at Stony Point.

214

215

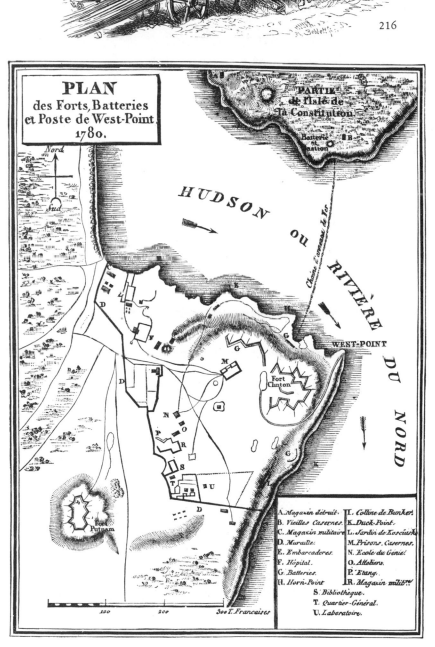

216

217

BENEDICT ARNOLD AND WEST POINT. FIG. 214: A view of West Point in 1780. Arnold obtained command of the fort in August, 1780. By late September his negotiations with the British were complete. Arnold was to betray the fort and its 3,000-man garrison for a large sum of money and high rank in the British army. British control of the fort, key to the Hudson, might have significantly altered the future course of the war. FIG. 215: Benedict Arnold. FIG. 216: Darley's drawing of Arnold's expedition through the Maine wilderness to Quebec in 1775. Although Arnold's efforts to capture Quebec came to nothing when he and General Richard Montgomery were repulsed outside the city on December 31, 1775, his leadership of the expedition was one of the accomplishments that would have preserved Arnold's reputation as an extraordinary field general if he had not turned traitor in 1780. FIG. 217: West Point in 1780, showing the position of the great chain which was strung across the river to block shipping.

*Head Quarters Robinsons
House Sep.r 22d. 1780

Permit Mr. John Anderson to pass the
Guards to the White Plains, or below
it if He chuses. He being on Public
Business by my Direction

B. Arnold M Genl*

ARNOLD AND ANDRÉ. Fig. 218: Major John André, in a sketch he made of himself the night before he was hanged. Fig. 219: André from another miniature portrait by himself. André was in charge of intelligence for the British in New York. In late September, 1780, he traveled to West Point to receive the plans of West Point and other confidential information from Arnold. Fig. 220: A facsimile of the pass which Arnold gave André to get him safely through the Westchester no-man's-land back to New York. Fig. 221: Major Benjamin Tallmadge, Washington's Chief of Intelligence, the first to realize what had been happening after André was captured with the incriminating documents. Even so he was not fast enough to prevent Arnold's escape.

FIG 222: André about to be captured by American militia-
mer. This illustration appeared in *Harper's Weekly*, October 2, 1880, a hundred years after the event.

223

224

225

226

227

228

ARNOLD AND ANDRÉ (*Continued*). The capture of André became one of the most often illustrated events of the Revolution. Three representative examples are seen in FIGS. 223–225. The documents were found in André's boots. Soon after his capture, André gave up pretending he was one John Anderson, the name Arnold gave him on his pass, and admitted his identity. If he had been captured in uniform, André would have been held as a prisoner of war and probably exchanged. Captured in civilian clothes, he was unquestionably a spy under military law and subject to hanging. FIG. 226: Obverse and reverse of medal awarded the captors of André. FIG. 227: Darley's drawing of Benedict Arnold's escape to New York. FIG. 228: Darley's drawing of the execution of André.

229

ARNOLD AND ANDRÉ (*Continued*). FIG. 229: Chappel's engraving of the death warrant being read to André. The stoic fortitude with which André met his fate prompts a parallel with Nathan Hale. For his unsuccessful efforts, Benedict Arnold received 6,315 pounds sterling, and modest pensions for his wife and children. He became a British Brigadier and took a disappointingly minor role in a few battles on the British side.

THE BATTLE OF CAMDEN. Fig. 230: Engraving after Chappel's painting of the American defeat at the Battle of Camden, South Carolina, on August 16, 1780. With a stalemate in the North, the British turned to the South with success: Savannah was seized in December, 1778, and Charleston fell with 5,500 men in May, 1780. After the capture of Charleston, the British were free to turn to South Carolina and with the victory at Camden began to solidify their hold on that area.

231

232

233

234

GUERRILLA WARFARE IN THE SOUTH. Fig. 231: Chappel's painting of Francis Marion, the "Swamp Fox" who brilliantly led a small but effective guerrilla force that prevented Cornwallis from achieving control of South Carolina in the last years of the war. Fig. 232: A portrait of Marion based on a painting by T. Stothard. Fig. 233: A typical camp scene of Marion's men. Fig. 234: Marion and his irregulars in a South Carolina swamp.

235

236

237

GREENE'S CAMPAIGN. FIG. 235: General Nathanael Greene, who replaced Horatio Gates as commander of the Southern army in December, 1780, in an engraving after a portrait by Trumbull. Success came quickly to Greene, who sent Daniel Morgan, called from retirement for one last effort, to meet the British at the Cowpens in northern South Carolina on January 17, 1781. FIG. 236: An early view of the Battle of the Cowpens. FIG. 237: Darley's drawing of action at the Cowpens. FIG. 238: Medal awarded to Morgan for his efforts at the Cowpens. Morgan's brilliant leadership is generally credited with the victory over an 1,100-man force under the feared Colonel Banastre Tarleton. FIG. 239: Medal awarded to Greene after the Battle of Eutaw Springs later in 1781. Greene's famous description of his Southern campaign: "We fight, get beat, rise, and fight again," was characteristically modest. While many of his battles were hard-fought draws or even marginal losses, the over-all effect of the campaign was to force Cornwallis closer and closer to the fatal trap that awaited him at Yorktown.

238

239

240

THE BATTLE OF THE COWPENS. Fig. 240: A view of the Battle of the Cowpens, January 17, 1781, by John Andrew from *Ballou's Pictorial* of November 1, 1856. American forces are driving the British back with bayonets while the cavalry skirmishes in the background.

241

TOWARD YORKTOWN. FIG. 241: The British and
American armies met again at Guilford Court House,
North Carolina, on March 15, 1781. This picture is a
view of American cavalry under the command of Henry
"Light Horse Harry" Lee at Guilford. Though the battle
was technically a British victory, Cornwallis' army was
badly mauled.

243

Sᴿ HENRY CLINTON.

244

TOWARD YORKTOWN *(Continued)*. Fɪɢ. 242: The final battle of the Southern campaign before Yorktown, at Eutaw Springs, South Carolina, on September 8, 1781, where the British fought Greene to a final costly draw. At the end of 1781, Cornwallis had been defeated at Yorktown, and all the British had left in the South were the ports of Charleston and Savannah. Fɪɢ. 243: General Charles Cornwallis, British commander at Yorktown, from a portrait by John Singleton Copley. Fɪɢ. 244: Sir Henry Clinton, British Commander-in-Chief in America. As Washington's army and the French troops under Comte de Rochambeau moved south from Newport toward New York in the summer of 1781, Clinton ordered Cornwallis' army, then already in Virginia, to the port of Yorktown on Chesapeake Bay, in case Clinton should need reinforcements in New York. When Washington heard that the French West Indies fleet under de Grasse had sailed for Chesapeake Bay, a battle plan was formulated. Bypassing New York, the French-American army would march to Virginia to encounter Cornwallis. If the French fleet could get to the Chesapeake before the British fleet, and if the American army could get there before de Grasse's October 15 deadline for leaving the North American theatre, a crucial victory might be won. As history proved, both "ifs" paid off for the Americans. Fɪɢ. 245: Rochambeau, from a painting by Trumbull.

245

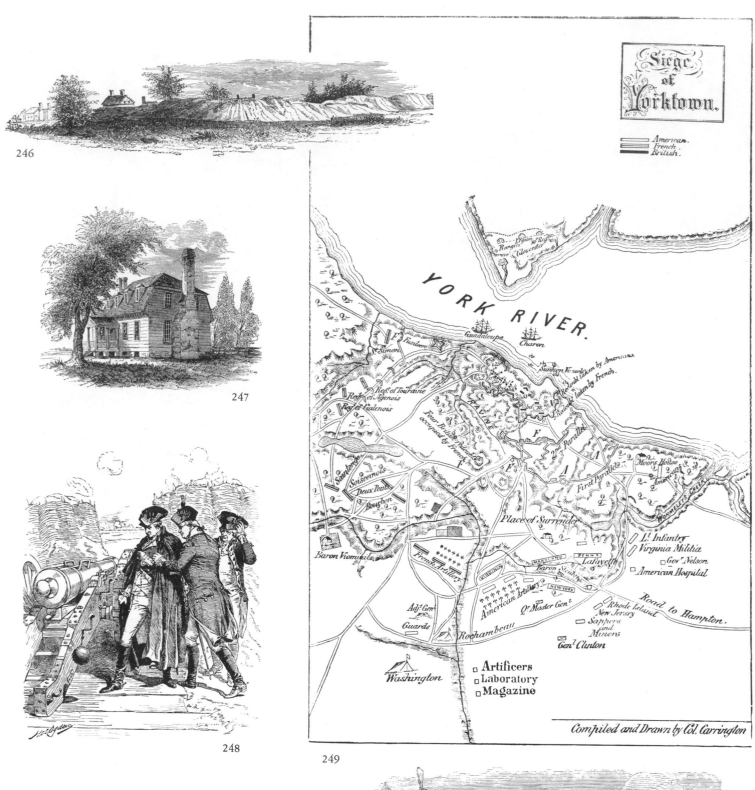

246

247

248

249

250

YORKTOWN: FIG. 246: Lossing's sketch of the British lines at Yorktown as they appeared c. 1850. FIG. 247: Mrs. Moore's house at Yorktown, where the surrender was arranged. FIG. 248: Scene in the American lines at Yorktown, as pictured by H. A. Ogden. The main American-French army reached Yorktown and laid siege to the British position on September 28. FIG. 249: Map of the siege of Yorktown. FIG. 250: Minor action around Yorktown as the Americans take a British redoubt.

Fɪɢ. 251: The climactic military action of the war — an engagement in which, ironically, no Americans took part — was the meeting of the French and British fleets off Cape Henry on September 5, 1781. The engagement is shown as drawn by J. O. Davidson for *Harper's Weekly's* commemorative issue of September 5, 1881.

Here the French secured control of the sea off Yorktown, leaving the British fleet no choice but to head north. As the American and French armies continued to pound the British position, surrender of Cornwallis' army became only a question of time.

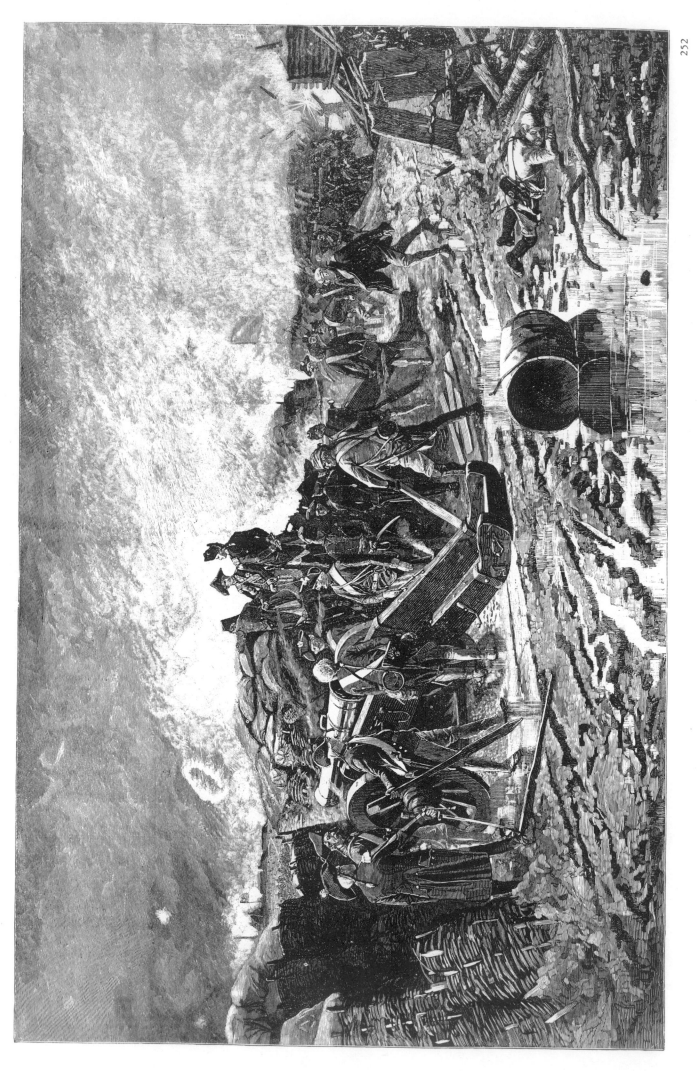

YORKTOWN (*Continued*). FIG. 252: A scene drawn by Rufus F. Zogbaum for *Harper's Weekly*, October 22, 1881, showing Washington inspecting the French batteries in the trenches at Yorktown. The American-French army of 16,000 men shelled the British position incessantly with 52 pieces of artillery. The storming of two British redoubts on October 14 shut off any slim hope of escape for the British army, and on October 17 Cornwallis wrote to Washington asking for a cease-fire so that a surrender could be discussed. On the afternoon of October 19, the British marched out of their position and laid down their arms.

253

254

FIG. 253: This mid-nineteenth-century conception of Cornwallis' surrender has similarities to the slightly later view shown in FIG. 254, in which a French officer is pointing out Washington to a figure no doubt meant to represent Cornwallis. In actuality, Cornwallis did not appear but sent an adjutant, Thomas O'Hara, to hand over the ceremonial sword indicating surrender. Seeing a British Brigadier approaching him with the sword, Washington, always alert to breaches of protocol and feeling that he, as Commander-in-Chief, could not accept a sword from a Brigadier, nominated General Benjamin Lincoln to receive the sword. The scene was accurately drawn by Darley (FIG. 256).

YORKTOWN AND THE END OF THE WAR.
Fig. 255: Howard Pyle's view of the surrender at Yorktown appeared in *Harper's Weekly* on October 22, 1881.

256

257

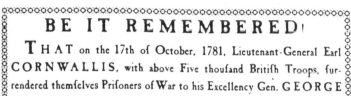

259

258

260

FIG. 256: Darley's account of the Yorktown surrender. Lincoln did not actually take the sword, but only placed his hand on it briefly, symbolizing the act of accepting the British surrender. FIGS. 257 and 260: Messengers such as these spread the news of Cornwallis' surrender throughout the colonies. FIGS. 258–259: Broadsides also spread the word. Yorktown of course did not immediately end the war. The British still had an army under Clinton in New York and another in South Carolina, and throughout the rest of 1781 and all of 1782 the American and British armies remained ready to strike at one another should the occasion arise. In late 1782, the British left South Carolina. On November 30, 1782, agreement was reached on the peace treaty, which was formally signed on September 3, 1783. In November, 1783, the British army left New York, and on November 25 the American army reentered the city which they had lost more than seven years before.

261

THE END OF THE WAR. Fig. 261: Howard Pyle's drawing of the Continental Army marching into New York.

DISBANDING OF THE CONTINENTAL ARMY. Fig. 262: H. A. Ogden's drawing from *Harper's Weekly*, October 20, 1883, commemorated the dis-banding of a major part of the Continental Army at New Windsor, New York, in early November, 1783.

263

264

265

THE END OF THE WAR. FIG. 263: Howard Pyle's drawing of the farewell dinner held by Washington and his officers at Fraunces' Tavern in New York. Pyle's drawing appeared in *Harper's Weekly*, December 4, 1883. FIG. 264: Fraunces' Tavern at Pearl and Broad Streets in New York, scene of the farewell dinner on December 4, 1783. FIG. 265: Darley's drawing of Washington's farewell to his officers.

FIG. 266: Washington resigning his commission as Commander-in-Chief. FIG. 267: Celebrating the adoption of the new Constitution of the United States in New York in 1788. FIG. 268: The scene at Federal Hall, New York, overlooking Wall and Broad Streets where Washington was inaugurated as President on April 29, 1789.

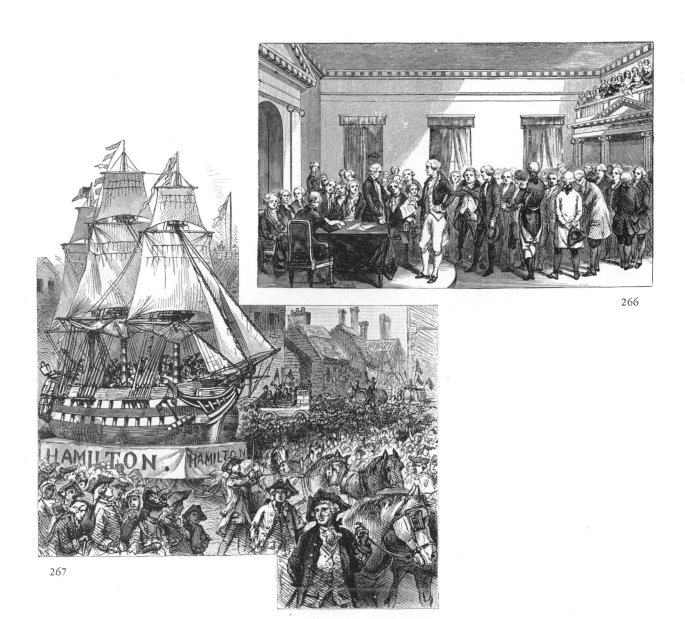

266

267

268

THE STATE HOUSE, PHILADELPHIA, WHERE THE CONVENTION WAS HELD.

WASHINGTON'S HOUSE, HIGH STREET, PHILADELPHIA.

ALEXANDER HAMILTON.

JAMES MADISON.

CHARLES COTESWORTH PINCKNEY.

ROGER SHERMAN.

BENJAMIN FRANKLIN.

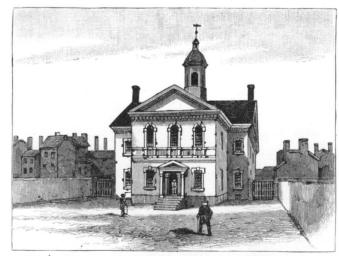

CARPENTER'S HALL, PLACE OF MEETING OF THE FIRST CONTINENTAL CONGRESS.

ELBRIDGE GERRY.

269

THE END OF THE WAR (*Continued*). FIG. 269:
A hundred years after the Constitutional Convention of
1787, this page appeared in *Leslie's Magazine* commemo-
rating the centennial of the Constitution.

THE DEFENDER OF THE MOTHERS WILL BE THE PROTECTOR OF THE DAUGHTERS

1776 1777

Fɪɢ. 270: An illustration depicting Washington's triumphant reception in Trenton, scene of one of his greatest victories, while en route to his inauguration in New York in 1789.

270

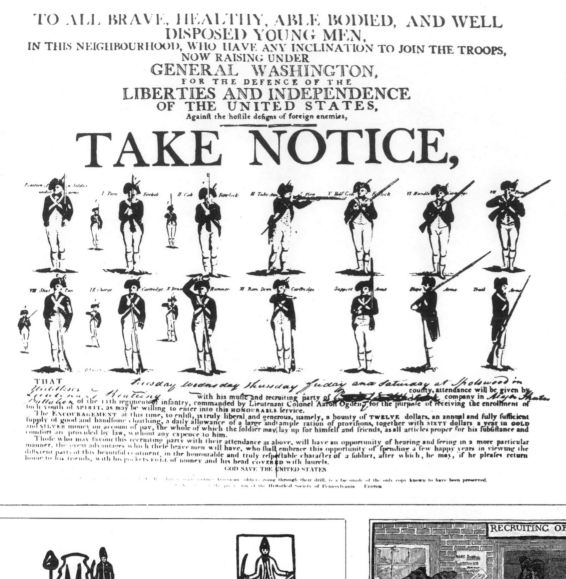

TO ALL BRAVE, HEALTHY, ABLE BODIED, AND WELL
DISPOSED YOUNG MEN,
IN THIS NEIGHBOURHOOD, WHO HAVE ANY INCLINATION TO JOIN THE TROOPS,
NOW RAISING UNDER
GENERAL WASHINGTON,
FOR THE DEFENCE OF THE
LIBERTIES AND INDEPENDENCE
OF THE UNITED STATES,
Against the hostile designs of foreign enemies,

TAKE NOTICE,

271

GREAT
ENCOURAGEMENT
FOR
SEAMEN.

ALL GENTLEMEN SEAMEN and able-bodied LANDSMEN
who have a Mind to distinguish themselves in the GLORIOUS
CAUSE of their COUNTRY, and make their Fortunes, an Op-
portunity now offers on board the Ship RANGER, of Twenty
Guns, (for FRANCE) now laying in PORTSMOUTH, in the State of NEW-HAMP-
SHIRE, commanded by JOHN PAUL JONES Esq; let them repair to the Ship's Rendez-
vous in PORTSMOUTH, or at the Sign of Commodore MANLEY, in SALEM, where they will be kind-
ly entertained, and receive the greatest Encouragement.---The Ship RANGER, in the Opinion of
every Person who has seen her is looked upon to be one of the best Cruizers in AMERICA.---She
will be always able to Fight her Guns under a most excellent Cover ; and no Vessel yet built
was ever calculated for sailing faster, and making good Weather.

Any GENTLEMEN VOLUNTEERS who have a Mind to take an agreable Voyage in this pleasant
Season of the Year, may, by entering on board the above Ship RANGER, meet with every
Civility they can possibly expect, and for a further Encouragement depend on the first Op-
portunity being embraced to reward each one agreable to his Merit.

All reasonable Travelling Expences will be allowed, and the Advance-Money be paid on
their Appearance on Board.

In CONGRESS, MARCH 29, 1777.

RESOLVED,

THAT the MARINE COMMITTEE be authorised to advance to every able Seaman, that
enters into the CONTINENTAL SERVICE, any Sum not exceeding FORTY DOL-
LARS, and to every ordinary Seaman or Landsman, any Sum not exceeding TWEN-
TY DOLLARS, to be deducted from their future Prize-Money.

By Order of CONGRESS,
JOHN-HANCOCK, PRESIDENT.

272

273

REVOLUTIONARY RECRUITING. FIG. 271: A
1799 recruiting poster when war threatened with France
illustrates poses from a manual of arms typical of the
Revolutionary period. FIG. 272: A naval recruiting
poster calling for men to serve on John Paul Jones' ship
"Ranger." FIG. 273: Howard Pyle's drawing of a
Revolutionary recruiting office in New London, from
Harper's Magazine, December, 1879.

274

275

276

277

JOHN PAUL JONES. FIG. 274: Engraving after Alonzo Chappel's painting of John Paul Jones, most famous American naval commander of the Revolution. FIG. 275: A British print of the period illustrating what was probably an apocryphal incident, that of Jones shooting a sailor who had attempted to strike his ship's colors during a battle. FIG. 276: A miniature portrait of John Paul Jones. FIG. 277: Darley's drawing of Jones encouraging his men.

278

279

280

DON'T TREAD ON ME

BON HOMME RICHARD & SERAPIS

281

JOHN PAUL JONES (*Continued*). FIG. 278: Chappel's engraving of Jones capturing the British ship "Serapis." Jones' ship, the "Bonhomme Richard," named by him in honor of Benjamin Franklin and *Poor Richard's Almanac,* met the "Serapis" on September 23, 1779, off Scarborough in the North Sea. After a three-and-one-half-hour battle, the "Serapis" surrendered while on fire. The "Bonhomme Richard" itself sank two days later, the ship's cause not having been helped by another American commander who fired indiscriminately at both ships as they battled. Hundreds of men on both ships were killed and wounded. The battle was not of much military significance, but became one of those psychologically important moments which produced a great deal of nineteenth-century illustration. FIG. 279: Obverse and reverse of medal awarded to Jones. FIG. 280: The capture of the "Serapis." FIG. 281: Illustration of the battle between the "Bonhomme Richard" and the "Serapis" published in *Ballou's Pictorial* on March 3, 1855. The "Bonhomme Richard" may be seen flying the rattlesnake flag while the illustration is bordered with that early American symbol.

283

284

282

285

286

288

FOREIGN OFFICERS IN THE AMERICAN REVOLUTION. FIG. 282: Tadeusz Andrzej Bonawentura Kosciuszko, Polish patriot who entered the Continental Army in 1776 as a volunteer, served at Saratoga and later designed the fortifications at West Point. FIG. 283: A Barber woodcut of the death of Baron de Kalb, who came to America with Lafayette and was killed at Camden. FIGS. 284–285: Casimir Pulaski was another Polish patriot who met Franklin in Paris in 1776. Franklin sent him to Washington, and Pulaski served in the American army at the Brandywine and Germantown and in the Southern campaigns. He was fatally wounded at Savannah in 1779. His banner is shown in FIG. 284. FIG. 286: Darley drew this illustration of the death of

Pulaski (actually Pulaski briefly survived the battle, but died of his wounds on shipboard shortly thereafter). FIG. 287: Pulaski's final cavalry charge at Savannah. FIG. 288: Portrait by Alonzo Chappel of the most famous foreign officer to serve with Washington, Marie Joseph Paul Yves Roch Gilbert du Motier, Marquis de Lafayette. Lafayette served at the Brandywine, Monmouth, and in the final Southern campaign and became one of Washington's closest friends. Though totally without experience when he arrived in America, Lafayette soon became a capable officer. Had he not been replaced by Charles Lee as commander of the attacking force at Monmouth at the last moment, the near miss that ensued might have turned out a major American victory.

289

FOREIGN OFFICERS IN THE AMERICAN
REVOLUTION *(Continued)*. Fig. 289: Chappel's
engraving of de Kalb introducing Lafayette to Silas Deane,
American diplomat in Paris.

290

291

WASHINGTON'S GENERALS. FIG. 290: Chappel's portrait of General Henry Knox. Knox, a bookseller active in the colonial militia, joined the Continental Army at Cambridge, Massachusetts, in 1775. Largely because of his knowledge of military literature, he was commissioned a Colonel and put in charge of artillery. After bringing from Ticonderoga the artillery that forced the British out of Boston, Knox served at Trenton, Princeton, Germantown, Monmouth, and Yorktown. He rose to the rank of Major General and was Secretary of War in Washington's first cabinet. FIG. 291: Chappel's portrait of General Benjamin Lincoln. Lincoln served primarily in the Southern campaign, and was forced to surrender his army at Charleston in 1780. Perhaps because of this, though he was not responsible for the loss of that city, Washington had Lincoln receive the ceremonial sword of surrender at Yorktown. FIG. 292: General Horatio Gates, after a painting by Gilbert Stuart. Gates was a veteran of the French and Indian War and commander of the army that defeated Burgoyne at Saratoga, though real credit for that victory must go to others—Stark, Schuyler, Morgan and, ironically, Benedict Arnold. After the collapse of the famous Conway Cabal that wanted to replace Washington with Gates in 1778, Gates served in the South where his disastrous defeat at Camden led to his being replaced by the most able of Washington's generals, Nathanael Greene.

292

WASHINGTON'S GENERALS *(Continued)*. FIG.
293: Obverse and reverse of medal awarded to Gates
after Saratoga. FIG. 294: General John Glover, after
a drawing by Trumbull. Glover was the commander of
the Marblehead mariners, an able company of seamen
who saved Washington's army in the evacuation of
Brooklyn Heights and negotiated the crossing of the
Delaware before the battle at Trenton. FIG. 295: General Israel Putnam, another veteran of the French and
Indian War, who, according to legend, left his plow
standing in his field to go to Cambridge on hearing the
news of Lexington and Concord. He served at Bunker
Hill and Long Island, but a stroke ended his career in
1779.

296

297

REVOLUTIONARY FIGURES. Fig. 296: Robert Morris, after a portrait by Chappel. Morris was the Philadelphia financier who did more than anyone else to keep the shaky finances of the Continental Congress and its army above water during the difficult war years, not least when he arranged for the funds which enabled Washington to transport his army from New York to Yorktown. Fig. 297: Thomas Paine, after a portrait by Romney. Paine's famous pamphlet, *Common Sense,* published early in 1776, did much to stimulate public opinion in favor of independence from England and expressed many ideas incorporated by Jefferson in the Declaration. A later pamphlet, *The Crisis,* helped hold the army together after the disaster of Long Island. Fig. 298: John Trumbull, in an engraving by Asher B. Durand after a painting by Waldo and Jewett. Trumbull, "painter of the Revolution," served in the Connecticut militia and as an aide to George Washington. Studying art in London, Trumbull was briefly imprisoned in retaliation for the hanging of André. During the first decades of the nineteenth century he painted the great historical scenes which defined many of the images left us by the Revolution.

298

299

300

301

THE CONSTITUTION. Figs. 299–301: The three authors of *The Federalist* papers, the series of essays which swayed opinion in favor of adoption of the Constitution in 1787–88. Fig. 299: Alexander Hamilton, from a miniature by Archibald Robertson. Fig. 300: James Madison, from a portrait by Gilbert Stuart. Fig. 301: John Jay, in an engraving by Asher B. Durand from a portrait by Stuart and Trumbull.

302

303

GEORGE WASHINGTON. FIG. 302: A version of the earliest portrait of Washington, an engraving after a painting made in 1772 by Charles Willson Peale. Washington is wearing the uniform he wore during the French and Indian War. FIG. 303: Washington, after a portrait by Rembrandt Peale. FIG. 304: Washington, after a Gilbert Stuart portrait.

304

GEORGE WASHINGTON *(Continued)*. Fig. 305:
Another version of Washington, after a Stuart portrait.
The miniature battle scene below the portrait depicts
the American army attacking at Trenton. Fig. 306:
Washington in uniform from a mid-nineteenth-century
illustration based on a Trumbull painting of Washington at Trenton.

GEORGE WASHINGTON *(Continued).* Fig. 307:
This illustration of a painting by Charles Willson Peale
depicting Washington at the end of the war was first
published in *Harper's Weekly* on May 4, 1889.

307

FIG. 308: Chappel's portrait of Washington.

309

310

311

312

313

314

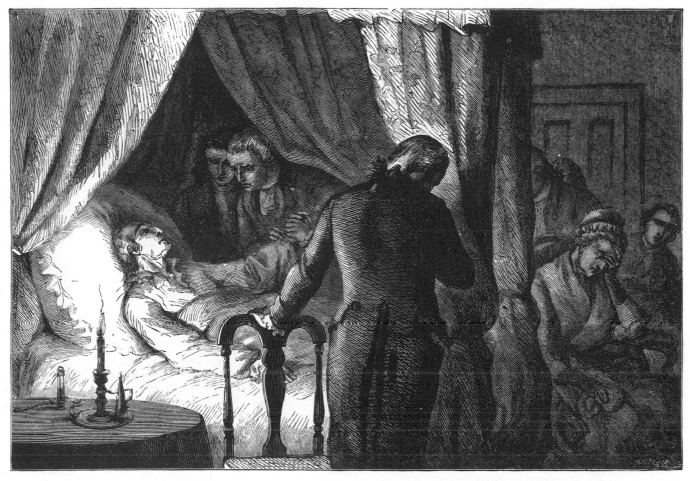

315

GEORGE WASHINGTON *(Continued)*. Fig. 309:
A silhouette of Washington. Figs. 310–311: Two views
of Mount Vernon. Fig. 312: Washington's book plate.
Fig. 313: Washington's camp chest. Fig. 314: Washington's sword. Fig. 315: Darley's drawing of the death
of Washington. Fig. 316: A miniature portrait of
Martha Washington.

316

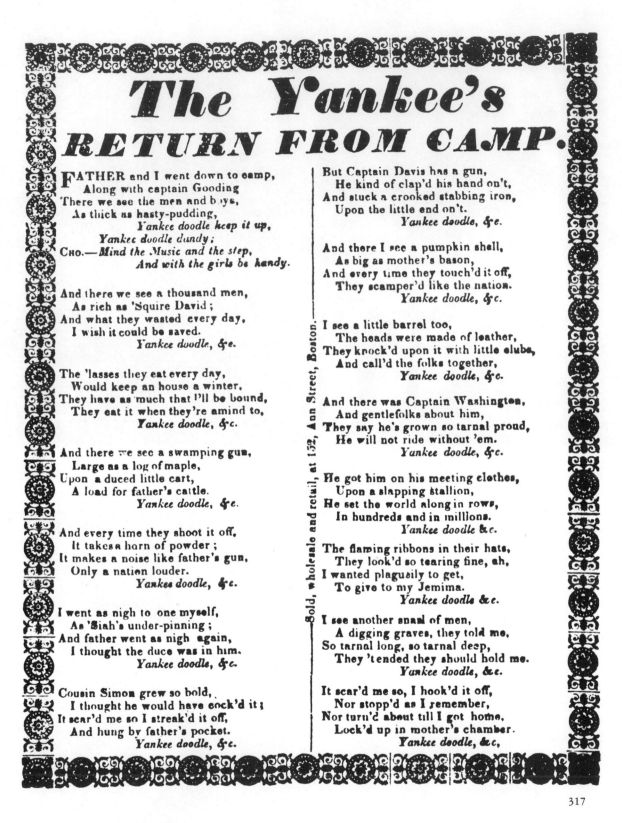

317

REVOLUTIONARY SOLDIERS. Fig. 317: An early
version of "Yankee Doodle."

318

Fig. 318: Engraving after a commemorative painting of an American soldier of the Revolution by George W. Maynard entitled simply " '76" and published in *Harper's Weekly* on July 15, 1876.

319

REVOLUTIONARY SOLDIERS *(Continued)*. Fig. 319: Illustration by Julian Scott entitled "Dangerous Ground" depicts a group of American soldiers on patrol in Indian territory during the Revolution. It was published in *Harper's Weekly* on May 13, 1876.

MANUAL OF ARMS. Figs. 320–327: The illustrations on pages 135 and 136 reproduce engravings from a mid-eighteenth-century manual of arms which was published both in England and in the colonies. As the colonial militia drilled on the English pattern, the exercises reproduced here may be taken as typical of the drill routines of both the regular English troops and their colonial opponents at the outset of the Revolution. We may assume, however, that the English professionals executed them with more precision than the amateur colonials.

1 Take Care.　　2 Join your Right-Hand to your Firelock.　　3 Poise your Firelock.
320　4 Join your Left-Hand to your Firelock.　　5 Cock your Firelock.　　6 Present. Fire.

7. Recover your Arms. See Fig. 12. Halfcock your Firelock.　　8. Handle your
Primer.　9. Prime, the first Motion.　10. Prime, the last Motion.　11. Shut your
Pan.　12. Cast about to charge, the first Motion.　　　　　　　　　　321

13 Cast about to charge.　　14 Handle your Cartridge.　　15 Open your Cartridge
16 Charge with Cartridge.　　17 Draw your Rammer, the first Motion.　　18 Draw
322　your Rammer, the last Motion.

19 Shorten your Rammer, the first Motion.　　20 Shorten your Rammer.　　21 Put
them in the Barrel.　　22 Ram down your Charge.　　23 Recover your Rammer
323　Shorten your Rammer. See Fig. 19.　　24 Return your Rammer.

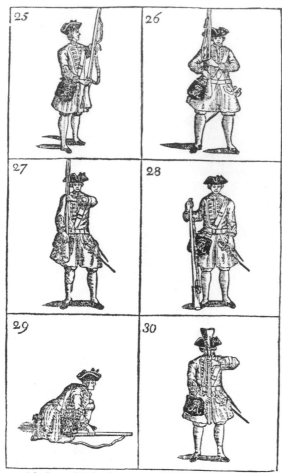

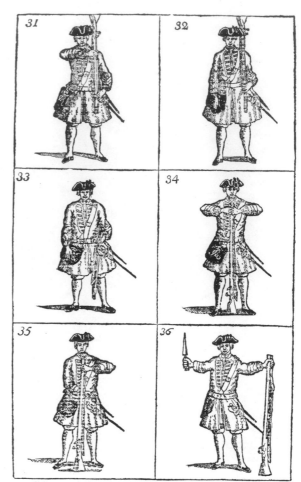

25. Cast off your Firelock. *See Fig.* 13. Your right Hand under your **Lock.**
26. Poise. *See Fig.* 2. Shoulder. *See Fig.* 1. Rest your Firelock. 27. Order your
Firelock, *the first Motion.* 28. Order your Firelock, *the last Motion.* 29. Ground
your Firelock. Take up your Firelock. *See Fig.* 28. 30. Rest. *See Fig.* 26. Club.
your Firelock, *the first Motion.*

31. Club your Firelock, *the third Motion.* 32. Club your Firelock, *the last Motion.*
33. Rest. *See Fig.* 26. Secure your Firelock. 34. Shoulder. *See Fig.* 1. Poise.
See Fig. 3. Rest on your Arms. 35. Draw your Bayonet, *the first Motion.* 36. Draw
your Bayonet.

37 Fix your Bayonet. 38 Rest your Bayonet. 39 Charge your Bayonet
Breaft-high, *the second Motion.* 40 Charge your Bayonet Breaft-high. 41 Push
your Bayonet. 42 Recover your Bayonet.

43 Rest your Bayonet on your Left Arm. 44 Rest, *see Fig.* 26. Shoulder, *see*
Fig. 1. Present your Arms. 45 To the Right 4 Times. 46 To the Right about.
47 To the Left as you were, *see Fig.* 44. To the Left 4 Times. 48 To the Left
about, *see Fig.* 46. To the Right as you were, *see Fig.* 44. Poise, *see Fig.* 3. Rest
on your Arms, *see Fig.* 34. Unfix your Bayonet. Return your Bayonet, *see Fig.* 35.
Poise, *see Fig.* 3. Shoulder, *see Fig.* 1.

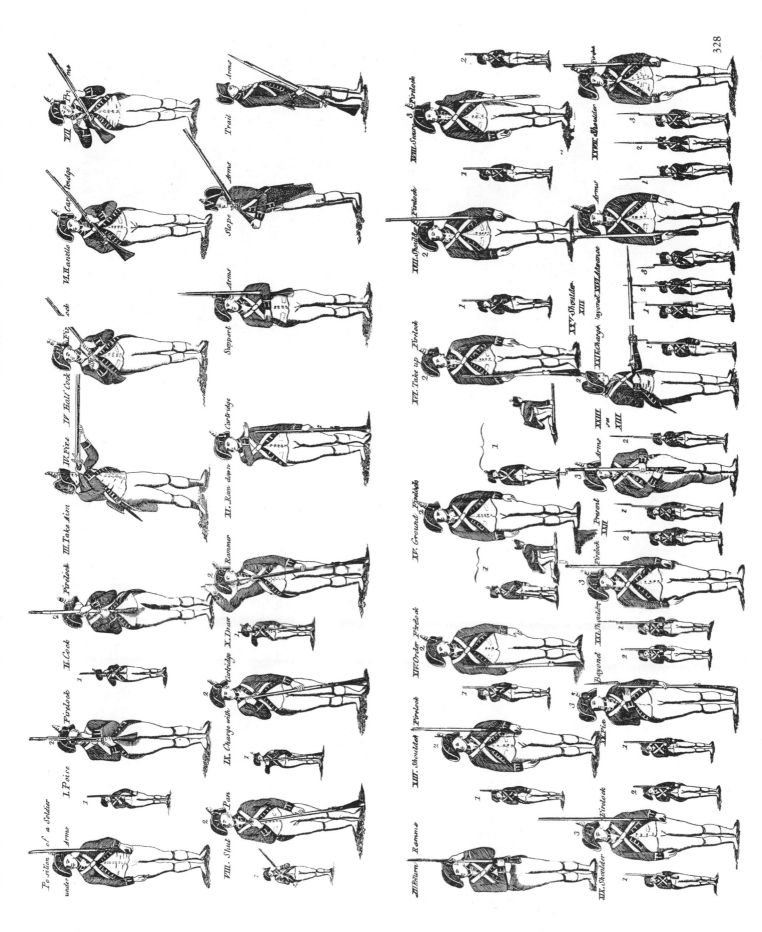

MANUAL OF ARMS (*Continued*). Fig. 328: Illustrations from an 1802 American manual of arms showing the drill exercises of the Continental soldiers.

330

329

331

332

333

334

AMERICAN AND BRITISH SOLDIERS OF
THE REVOLUTION. FIG. 329: An American soldier
drawn by Darley. FIG. 330: French and American uniforms. FIG. 331: Uniforms of the British army during
the Revolutionary period. FIG. 332: An American rifle-
man. FIG. 333: A British Grenadier. FIG. 334: An
American soldier.

335

336

337

THE HESSIANS IN THE REVOLUTION. Fig.
335: Darley's drawing of German soldiers being drafted
for service in America. During the period from 1776 to
1783 as many as 17,000 German mercenary soldiers—
primarily from the state of Hesse-Cassel, thus the name
Hessians—fought for the British in America. Fig. 336:
A Hessian troop marching. Fig. 337: A Hessian Grenadier. Fig. 338: Hessians being routed by American soldiers.

338

339

340

341

342

343

344

SCENES FROM THE REVOLUTION. FIG. 339: A British troop movement across New Jersey. FIG. 340: Morgan's riflemen in action. FIG. 341: Militiamen crossing a mountain. FIG. 342: A cavalry battle. FIG. 343: A council of war on horseback. FIG. 344: American soldiers.

345

346

347

348

349

350

FIG. 345: Hand-to-hand combat. FIG. 346: Chopping trees to obstruct the British march. FIG. 347: Moving a cannon into position. FIG. 348: British troops and Indians with an American prisoner. FIG. 349: British soldiers destroying livestock. FIG. 350: British troops plundering.

SCENES FROM THE REVOLUTION *(Continued)*. Fig. 351: A Howard Pyle vignette of American soldiers. Fig. 352: A spy hanged by American soldiers. Fig. 353: An American mortar surrounded by a section of the chain originally strung across the Hudson at West Point. Fig. 354: A wounded American officer directing a battle.

351

352

353

354

355

356

INDIANS AND THE FRONTIER. Fig. 355: Darley's drawing of Indians and their prisoners in Pennsylvania's Wyoming Valley. Fig. 356: George Rogers Clark, in an engraving after a portrait by J. W. Jarvis. While the Revolution was fought out in coastal areas, Americans continued to battle the British and their Indian allies on the interior frontier. Clark's capture of Vincennes in 1779 after an epic march through flooded wilderness gave the Americans control over the huge "Old Northwest" Territory — modern Ohio, Indiana and Illinois.

357

358

359

INDIANS AND THE FRONTIER *(Continued)*.
Fig. 357: Mohawk chief Joseph Brant. The main area
of Indian activity during the Revolutionary period was
western New York and Pennsylvania where the Six
Nations of the Iroquois and their British allies battled
American settlers and villages. Fig. 358: Battle with the
Indians. An American army broke the power of the Six
Nations during a campaign in the summer of 1779. Fig.
359: Most famous Indian atrocity of the Revolution, the
murder of Jane McCrea by Burgoyne's Indians in 1777.
Fig. 360: Americans burning an Indian village.

360

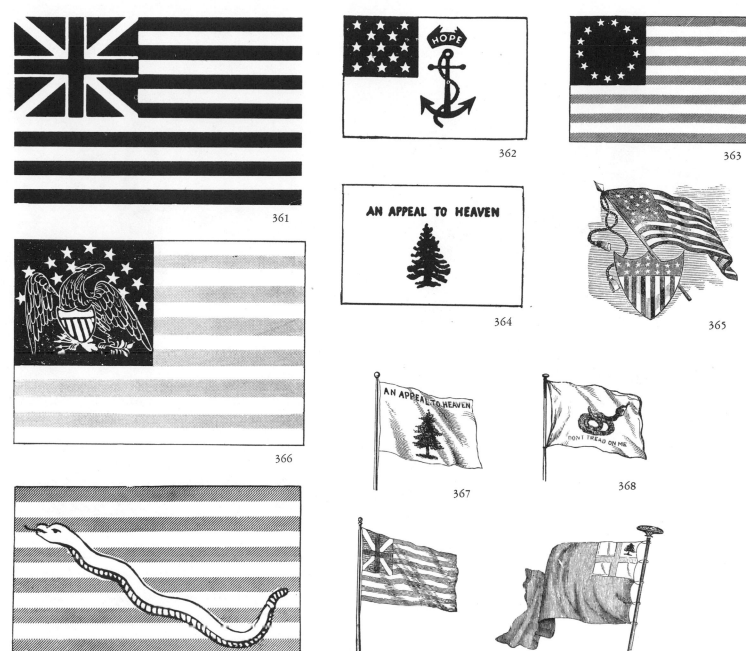

FLAGS OF THE REVOLUTION. Fig. 361: The Grand Union Flag, America's first official flag with thirteen stripes symbolizing the Thirteen Colonies. Fig. 362: Naval flag of Rhode Island with thirteen stars. Fig. 363: An early version of the Stars and Stripes. Fig. 364: Pine Tree flag of New England. Fig. 365: Flag and shield. Fig. 366: Flag of a Continental regiment at Yorktown. Figs. 367–368: The Pine Tree flag and a variant of the rattlesnake flag. Fig. 369: South Carolina naval flag with the rattlesnake motif. Fig. 370: Another view of the Union flag. Fig. 371: Another variant of the New England flag. Fig. 372: New York Regimental flag, 1778.

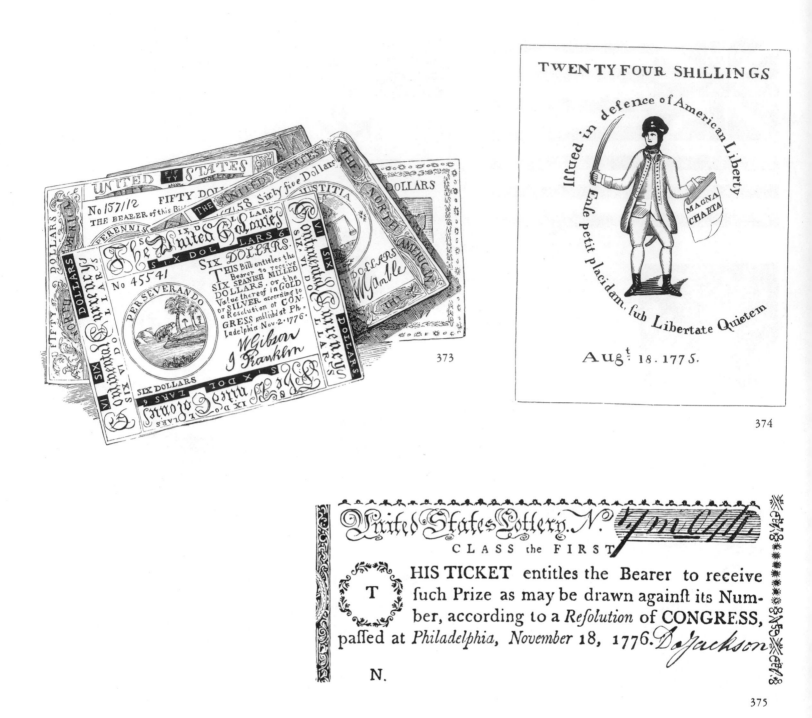

REVOLUTIONARY FINANCE. FIG. 373: Continental paper money. FIG. 374: A Massachusetts treasury note of 1775. FIG. 375: A United States lottery ticket of 1776. FIG. 376: Facsimiles of Continental coins.

377

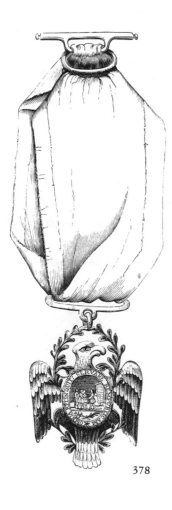

379

THE SOCIETY OF THE CINCINNATI. FIG.
377: Members' Certificate of the Society of the Cincinnati, an organization founded in 1783 for Revolutionary
soldiers and their descendants. FIG. 378: The order of
the Cincinnati. FIG. 379: The Great Seal of the United
States, approved by Congress in 1782.

378

DELAWARE.

380

PENNSYLVANIA.

381

NEW JERSEY.

382

383

GEORGIA.

384

[He who transplanted still sustains.]

CONNECTICUT.

385

[By the sword he seeks peace under Liberty.]

MASSACHUSETTS.

386

MARYLAND.

387

SOUTH CAROLINA

388

[Thus always with tyrants.]

VIRGINIA.

389

[More Elevated.]

NEW YORK.

390

NEW HAMPSHIRE.

391

NORTH CAROLINA.

392

RHODE ISLAND.

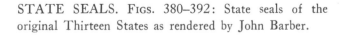

STATE SEALS. FIGS. 380–392: State seals of the original Thirteen States as rendered by John Barber.

148

EAGLES. Figs. 393–409: Eagles and other patriotic
devices reproduced from early American examples.

397

398

399

400

401

402

403

404

405

406

407

408

409

410

INDEPENDENCE DAY. Fɪɢ. 410: The Centennial
152 celebration of the Declaration of Independence as observed at Independence Hall in Philadelphia on July 4, 1876, and illustrated in *Harper's Weekly* on July 22, 1876.

411

FIG. 411: A nineteenth-century Independence Day celebration drawn by Gilbert Gaul.